FRANK STAGG

THE HOLY SPIRIT TODAY

BROADMAN PRESS   NASHVILLE, TENNESSEE

Library of Congress Catalog Card Number: 73-85701
Dewey Decimal Classification: 231.3
Printed in the United States of America

DEDICATED TO THE MEMORY OF
W. HERSEY DAVIS
AND IN APPRECIATION OF
EDWARD A. McDOWELL
MY TEACHERS IN THE
GREEK NEW TESTAMENT

CONTENTS

PREFACE

This book came to birth not so much through "planned parent-hood" but through the conjunction of my personal needs and current waves of interest and practice. A cluster of questions and problems as well as gains and opportunities center around deep and wide-spread concern today with the Holy Spirit. My own disposition has been to back off from what seemed to me to be certain superficial and often erratic preoccupations and practices in the name of the Holy Spirit.

Two motives drove me to the study and effort behind this book: (1) the concern to understand various movements, beliefs, and practices in the Christian community and (2) concern for a more informed, biblically oriented understanding of the Holy Spirit for my personal needs as well as for the church and the world today.

The first and most important question is the biblical meaning of the Holy Spirit as it bears upon the biblical understanding of God. This takes us directly to the "trinitarian" question. With due respect for the early "fathers" and for the great councils which struggled for clarity of understanding and statement, this book is offered in the firm conviction that we must keep going back to Scripture itself for our understanding of what is meant by the Holy Spirit, including the meaning of this for the doctrine of God. I have not found traditional statements formulated by the church to speak with clarity to me, and I find little evidence that people in the churches have found our "explanations" to be clear or very meaningful. Some give up as hopeless the effort to hold together the oneness of God and our knowledge of him as Father, Son, and Holy Spirit. Some seem to hold to a virtual tri-theism. What is offered here is not a final effort but a fresh effort to understand biblical intention.

There is great interest today in "faith healing" and in "tongues," both seen by many as prime manifestations of the Spirit. What about the many people of apparent faith and piety who suffer and die? What is the meaning of "tongues" in the New Testament, and what do they mean today? Do "tongues" follow the pattern of incarnation (the Word made flesh) or do they reverse the incarnation of the Word? Since boyhood I have had close relationship with friends who have esteemed and spoken in "tongues." Am I negligent or are they misguided? As an exegete it is my responsibility, whatever the measure of achievement, to understand the biblical evidence and intention. Hence the attention to these subjects, with a chapter devoted to each.

The crisis of impiety and the excessive claims of some to sinless perfection compel attention to the question of the holiness of the Spirit and the holiness which is his work to perform. With contempt for holiness on the one hand and proud claims to excellence on the other, where is the road that avoids both in favor of authentic piety? Must we choose between the loud voices for "law and order" and the strong inclination today toward permissiveness, or is there a *tertium quid?* Is there a biblically directed way which is neither legalistic or libertine, which offers freedom and moral-ethical responsibility at the same time?

Although this book deliberately challenges what it considers a misreading of the Holy Spirit and his work, its intention is not merely to protest. Its basic concern is to see the positive thrust of the Spirit of God into our world and into our existence, tracing from biblical perspective the many-sided work of the Spirit and the resultant fruit.

FRANK STAGG

The Beeches
Louisville, Kentucky

1 The Holy Spirit and the Oneness of God

Along with wide varieties in experience, beliefs, and practices of the people of God reflected in Scripture, there are basic non-negotiables in biblical perspective. These nonnegotiables include the oneness of God, his continuing presence in the world he has made, and the divine-human nature of Jesus Christ. It is in this context that the biblical doctrine of God is to be understood. It is in this context that the Holy Spirit is to be understood.

The oneness of God. Monotheism is so deeply embedded in the Bible that it forbids any theologizing which calls into question the oneness of God. The Old Testament reflects many struggles against both polytheism, the worship of more than one God by the same people, and henotheism, the acknowledgement of other gods but worship of one alone. Chemosh, Molech, Baal, and other gods were rejected in favor of one God alone, Yahweh. The first of the Ten Commandments may be directed against either polytheism or henotheism; but in either event, what is affirmed is that there is one God alone for our worship and service.

In the Old Testament the great concern with monotheism is not primarily in the context of metaphysical or theoretical debates. Rather it is on the plane of practical living. The prophets were concerned to destroy the power of false gods over Israel, whether formally recognized gods like Baal or Chemosh or gods like money, lust, greed, or pride. It was not so much that the prophets sought an orthodox creed, although this had importance. It was that they wanted the people of Israel to be freed from the power of these false gods and to give themselves wholly to the one true God. In either event, whether the concern was for orthodoxy or orthopraxy, the concern was for the acknowledgement of one and only one god.[1]

There is no more fundamental tenet for Judaism or Christianity than what is known as the *Shema* of Deuteronomy 6:4, which reads: "Hear, O Israel: the Lord our God is one Lord; and you shall love the Lord your God with all your heart, and with all your soul, and with all your might" (RSV). So basic is this confession that it is recurrent in the New Testament (cf. Mark 12:29 f.; Matt. 22:37; Luke 10:27; 1 Tim. 2:5). The oneness of God is explicit elsewhere (cf. 1 Cor. 8:6; John 17:3; Rom. 3:30; Gal. 3:20; 1 Tim. 1:17; Jude 25; Eph. 4:6; Jas. 2:19). It is as non-negotiable to the New Testament as to the Old. God is one God, not many, not three, not two, but one alone.

That the earliest Christians did not see themselves as compromising the monotheism of Judaism and that their Jewish contemporaries did not so accuse them is well attested. To begin with, Jesus and all of his earliest followers were Jews. They worshiped in the synagogues and the Temple in Jerusalem, and they were steeped in the Jewish Scriptures. At one time there were tens of thousands of Jews in Jerusalem who followed Jesus as the Christ, recognized the empowering presence of the Spirit of God, and yet believed in one God alone (cf. Acts 2:4,36,41; 4:4; 6:7; 21:20). For some decades Paul and his associates were permitted to preach Jesus as the Christ in synagogues (cf. Acts 9:20; 13:5,14,43; 14:1; 17:1,10,17; 18:4,19,26; 19:8). When evicted, it was not on the charge of compromising monotheism, but because of eroding or crossing the line between Jew and Gentile (cf. Acts 21:21,27-30; 22:21 f.; Gal. 2:11-14).

[1] I am indebted here to a colloquium paper "One God Alone," by Professor Ulrich W. Mauser, Presbyterian Theological Seminary, presented at The Southern Baptist Theological Seminary, Louisville, Kentucky (Spring, 1971).

Jesus Christ, God and Man. A second nonnegotiable is the union of God and man in Jesus Christ.[2] The deity and humanity of the incarnate word are affirmed without compromise of the oneness of God.

Even the strongest statement in the New Testament about Christ as mediator begins with a reaffirmation of the oneness of God: "For God is one, and there is one mediator of God and men, the man Christ Jesus" (1 Tim. 2:5). In the Greek text there is no word for "between," and to supply it, as is done in most translations, may obscure the intention of the verse.[3] The introduction could not be stronger: *"One* is God!" Then is the recognition of one mediator who is both of God and of men. He is human and divine. He is not a third party between God and men but rather one in whom God and men meet directly. In Jesus Christ is neither a link nor a wedge between God and men. He is the union of God and men. Jesus Christ is not a second God nor just a third of God. He is the eternal God uniquely present in a truly human life. This is what is meant by the incarnation, and it is in this sense that Jesus Christ is our mediator.

One may ask "But what about the prayers of Jesus?" Do they not imply some division in God? The answer is no. The prayers of Jesus belong to the mystery of incarnation, not to a three-fold division in God. Jesus Christ was truly human as well as divine, and out of his humanity he did pray. This is not to be understood as one God praying to another God, or one part of God praying to another part of God. It is to be understood as the prayers which came from an authentic human life, one in which

[2]Cf. John Knox, *The Humanity and Divinity of Christ* (Cambridge University Press, 1967) for a clear, concise tracing of New Testament Christological developments.

[3]The Greek syntax may imply "between," as in the Jewish apocryphal writing, *The Testament of Daniel* 6:2, but context here seems to call for our rendering, permitted but not required by Greek syntax. For the familiar reading with "between," see Martin Dibelius and Hans Conzelmann, *The Pastoral Epistles*, "Hermeneia" (Philadelphia: Fortress Press, 1972), pp. 41 f.

God was uniquely present as "the Word made flesh." We do not and need not "explain" the mystery of the incarnation; certainly there must be no disposition to remove it. We cannot "explain" Jesus Christ; we can have some understanding of him.

Like the prayers of Jesus, so does his cry on the cross suggest to some a division within God: "My God, my God, why hast thou forsaken me?" (Matt. 27:46). About a century ago, John A. Broadus put it this way: "If it be asked how he could feel himself to be forsaken, we must remember that a human soul as well as a human body was here suffering, a human soul thinking and feeling within human limitations (Mark 13:32), not psychologically unlike the action of other devout souls when in some great and overwhelming sorrow."[4] Again, the mystery is not overcome, but what is to be seen is the overwhelming loneliness of one who is truly human, even though also the Son of God.

The vision of Stephen, seeing "the Son of man standing on the right hand of God" (Acts 7:56), is another type of evidence cited by some to support the view of separate divine presences, but surely this is to put too much weight on highly symbolic language. "Anthropomorphic" language is the only kind of language man has, so he must speak of God in language which is taken from the experience of man. That God literally sits upon a throne, like an earthly monarch, is not the intention of Scripture. Such models as "throne" or "at the right hand" are symbolic ways of referring to sovereignty and power. The intention of Stephen's vision is not to represent a literal, physical relationship, but to communicate a most important truth: the very one whom wicked men had sought to destroy at Golgotha is the very power of God and lives on triumphantly. The Son of man is not a second God nor one third of God, but he is God in his sovereign power, both in judgment and redemption.

[4]John A. Broadus, *The Gospel of Matthew*, "An American Commentary on the New Testament" (Philadelphia: The American Baptist Publication Society, 1886), p. 574. Cf. also, Frank Stagg, "Matthew," *Broadman Bible Commentary* (Nashville: Broadman Press, 1969), vol. 8, pp. 245 f.

The continuing presence of God. A third nonnegotiable is the continuing presence of God. God created the world and continues his presence within it. He is not pantheistic. Pantheism sees the world and God as the same. He is not deistic, distant, and inaccessible to the world. Rather he is both before and above his world yet active within it. God is Spirit and may as such be worshiped anywhere in the world (John 4:24). He is Immanuel, God with us (Matt. 1:23). In sum, God is before all things and above all things as the one and only God. He also is ever present in his world, here in his nearness and power. He also has penetrated deeply into history and into his world, as deep as when the Word became flesh and dwelt among us (John 1:14).

Trinitarianism

The New Testament is content to know God as the eternal Father, as the Word made flesh in Jesus of Nazareth, and as the abiding nearness of the Holy Spirit. It does not attempt to work out a formal doctrine of trinity. This is the work of later generations of Christians. For New Testament faith, it is important to see what the New Testament says and what it does not say. It is important to see where the New Testament leaves off and where later Christian theologizing takes up, whether that theologizing be in the formulations of the Great Councils in early centuries, the Reformers, or this little book.

It was first in the second century that the "trinitarian question" was raised as such. The word "trinity" does not appear in the New Testament, and it is to be recognized that there is no formal doctrine of trinity in the New Testament.[5] Rather, it is that the faith of the New Testament finally compelled theology to seek a rationale for its belief in the oneness of God as well as the deity of Christ and presence of the Spirit of God.

[5]Students of the late W. O. Carver, Professor of Missions in The Southern Baptist Theological Seminary, will recall his clear thinking at this point.

The formal doctrine of trinity was rounded out in the fourth century, but its roots are older. Tertullian (A.D. 160?—230?) is credited with coining the word "*trinitas*," the Latin for "trinity," the unity of three: Father, Son, and Holy Spirit. Earlier, Theophilus had used the Greek term "triad."[6] The concern of Theophilus, Irenaeus, Tertullian, and others was to preserve faith in the oneness of God in the light of the recognition of the deity of Christ and reality of the Holy Spirit. But what began as insistence upon tri-*unity* eventually became an emphasis upon the threeness and increasing jeopardy to the belief in oneness.

A mistranslation of Colossians 2:9 added to the confusion. Paul declared that the fulness of "Godness" dwelt bodily in Christ. "Godness" or "Godhood" (*Theotēs*) came to be thought of as "Godhead." Then the head became heads, three in number. *Theotēs* is employed in Colossians to refute the gnostic doctrine that the *pleroma* (fulness) of deity is distributed over a hierarchy of angelic beings. The Gnostics built their theology on the premise that there is an ultimate dualism between spirit and matter, spirit alone being good and matter being inherently evil. This posed for them many problems, including that of the origin of the created world. How could a good God who is spirit create a material world? One answer was to fill the gap with a series of eons or emanations from God, the last of which was the **demiurge** (worker) and the total of which was the **pleroma** (fulness). Paul's opponents at Colossae seemed to give Jesus a place in this series, but that was not enough for Paul. He insisted that the fulness (*pleroma*) of deity (*theotes*) was in Christ himself and not in some hierarchy of angels. His term means "godness" or "deity," not "godhead" as it came to be understood.

To the term trinity were soon added the terms "persons," "three persons," "three persons of the Godhead," and even the ranking of the persons as first, second, and third. Thus trini-

[6]A. W. Wainwright, *The Trinity in the New Testament* (London: S.P.C.K., 1962), p. 4.

tarianism was fast on the way to tritheism, a de facto belief in three distinct gods. This the New Testament never anticipated and does not support.

The question before us is not the deity of Christ nor the reality of the Spirit of God. The question is not even the intention behind the emergence of the nonbiblical terms trinity and "godhead." The question concerns the adequacy of the term trinity and its related expressions to capture the New Testament understanding of God. It is binitarianism, belief in two gods, and tritheism, belief in three gods, which are to be challenged.

Moreover, there is here no sympathy at all with Unitarianism, the denial of the deity of Christ. We would insist that although the mystery of God whom we know as Father, Son, and Holy Spirit cannot and need not be dissolved, the New Testament faith does not have to choose between tritheism[7] and unitarianism. Both are to be resoundingly rejected in favor of New Testament faith. It is to be recognized that there is no neat, trinitarian pattern which does justice to the richness of the biblical understanding of God.[8] This present effort also will fall short, but it hopes at least to move the discussion closer to New Testament language and faith.

Whatever may have been gained as theology tried to move beyond New Testament statement, there have been many resultant problems. Outsiders, and apparently many within the church, get the impression that we hold to more than one god or at least to divisions within God. This borders on tritheism, a form of polytheism; and it opens the way to false ideas about the relationship between Father, Son, and Holy Spirit. Many seem to think that the Father is distant, harsh, or even hostile. The Son is thought of as nearer and more sympathetic. In some atonement theories

---

[7]Tritheism is used in distinction from trinity. The latter term seeks to maintain the oneness of God, whereas tritheism is used for the loss of this oneness.

[8]Cf. Cyril C. Richardson, *The Doctrine of the Trinity* (New York: Abingdon Press, 1958), p. 13.

the Son is seen as saving us from the wrath of God, somehow appeasing or satisfying him. The Father is seen in penal theories as punishing the Son, or even turning from him at Golgotha.[9] This contradicts the emphatic teaching of the New Testament that it is the Father's own presence and his own redeeming love which come to redemptive expression in the Son. It overlooks the fact that in Christ it is God who is reconciling the world to himself (2 Cor. 5:19).

Another unfortunate deduction from trinitarian formulations is the notion that the Holy Spirit is more spiritual than Father or Son. There is the erroneous idea that one can know the Son and yet not have the Spirit. This overlooks the fact that the Holy Spirit is the Spirit of God himself, and that only the Spirit of God can lead to a faith commitment to Jesus Christ (cf. 1 Cor. 12:3). Much fragmentation of the church into those who see themselves as super-Christians, having the Spirit in addition to Christ, grows out of this fragmentizing of God into three different, or even different kinds of persons.

An Attempted Restatement

God as absolute. The human mind can speak of absoluteness, but it does so out of intuition or logic and not out of experience or comprehension. In the nature of the case, the absolute is beyond human capacity. Man is finite and cannot comprehend the absolute. However, to infer absoluteness in God follows properly from the disclosures of Scripture and the necessities of faith. The first affirmation of Scripture speaks of God "in the beginning" (1:1). The idea of "beginning" is itself incomprehensible to man's finite mind. In biblical faith, however, God is in the beginning, before anything else. But the Bible is not interested in talking about God in his absoluteness or beyondness. It speaks of him in his relatedness, especially as creating, revealing, and redeeming. All three basic terms, Father, Son, and Holy Spirit, speak of God not in his beyondness but in his relation to us.

[9]See Broadus, *op. cit.*, p. 574 for a clear rejection of this idea.

The term for God's absoluteness is simply God. Yahweh is a personal name, as he came to be known to Israel. "Father" is the primary designation by which Jesus knew God (Luke 2:49) and by which he taught us to address him (Matt. 6:9). Sometimes "Father" is thought of as the term for God's absoluteness, but even this term sees him as he relates to his people. "Father" implies "children," so is a term of relationship. Of the terms Father, Son, and Holy Spirit, the first may sometimes seem to refer to God in his absoluteness, but each in some sense sees God only as in some way he relates to his people. When we seek to speak of God as before us, above us, and beyond us, the term in Scripture best suited to the intention is simply "God." God as Father, is God revealing himself, redeeming us, judging, sustaining, forgiving, and so forth.

Jesus Christ. Jesus Christ is God, but God as penetrating history and world, even to the extent of becoming uniquely present in the truly human existence of Jesus of Nazareth. Jesus Christ is God incarnate, yet God is prior to and more than God incarnate. This is clearly implied in the Gospel of John, where paradoxically Christ is identified with the Father and yet is less than the Father. Jesus said, "I and the Father are one" (John 10:30) and further, "The one having seen me has seen the Father" (14:9). The paradox follows in the further affirmation, "The Father is greater than I" (14:28). How may we, as we must, hold together all these claims?

Jesus Christ is God uniquely present in an actual human life. In Christ we encounter God himself, not just an emissary from God. In Jesus Christ God is doing his own speaking. He is doing his own deed. In Christ we have Immanuel (Matt. 1:23), God himself rather than his "foreign secretary." Paul declared that "God was in Christ," but God is before and beyond this presence in Jesus Christ.

Jesus Christ is God uniquely present in a truly human life, but he is not a second god nor only one third of God. Jesus Christ is the Word made flesh (John 1:1). The Word which became flesh was God, not the second person of the trinity. John does not say, "In the beginning was the Word, and the Word was with God, and the Word was the Second Person of the trinity" (1:1). He says that "the Word was God." Jesus Christ is more than "the Second person of the trinity"; He is Immanuel, *God* with us. Immanuel does not mean "the Second person of the trinity with us." Immanuel is *God with us*.

Jesus Christ is the Word made flesh. The Word is God creating, revealing, and redeeming. In his absoluteness and beyondness we cannot know God. In this sense, "No man has seen God at any time" (John 1:18). We know God in his relatedness, as he relates to us. The Word is God relating. It is in view of this that Jesus could declare the paradox: "The Father and I are one . . . the Father is greater than I." God in his absoluteness is greater than God relating to us.

The Holy Spirit. The Holy Spirit is the Spirit of God, not the Spirit of the third person of the trinity. The Holy Spirit is God in his nearness and power, anywhere and anytime, the very divine presence incarnated in Jesus Christ now present in his people. He is not a third God nor one-third of God. He is God himself relating to us in judgment, guidance, strength, redemption, or otherwise.

The Holy Spirit is not the spiritual side of God. He is not more spiritual than the Father or the Son. God is Spirit (John 4:24). It is not that the Holy Spirit alone is Spirit. The Holy Spirit did not first come at Pentecost, for the Old Testament and the Gospels also know of God's presence as the Spirit. The Holy Spirit is not the special possession of super Christians. He is God's presence in and with all his people. All of God's children may not have shoes, as the beloved "spiritual" has it in song, but all of God's children have the Holy Spirit, although some may not be aware of him.

The Holy Spirit, then, is not a third god nor one third of God. The Holy Spirit is God himself in his nearness and power, anytime and anywhere, the same divine presence as we know in the word made flesh, Immanuel.[10]

Someone will say, "But this is modalism." Labels come easy, and this label as widely employed is to be rejected, even though it is to be preferred to tritheism. If by "modalism" one means that God comes serially, now as Father, now as Son, and now as Holy Spirit, this is to be rejected as not doing justice to New Testament faith. That is the very fragmentation of God which this book sees as contrary to New Testament faith. That God may be known, and is actually known, as Father, Son, and Holy Spirit, is true to New Testament faith. But "modalism" as God divided or God coming in instalments is not true to New Testament faith.

Theology's problem is that it has no terms or models which do justice to the reality of God in the richness of his self-disclosure to us and his presence with us. Our point is that when we encounter God as Father, it is God himself (not a fraction) whom we meet. When we encounter God as Son, it is God himself who is with us. When we encounter God as Holy Spirit, it is God himself whom we encounter. This understanding of the oneness of God is of utmost importance in all that we are to understand about the Holy Spirit.

[10]For a forceful argument that the Gospel of John locates the activity of the Spirit within the church, the church itself incarnating the Spirit-Paraclete, see George Johnston, *The Spirit-Paraclete in the Gospel of John*, "Society for New Testament Studies Monograph Series," No. 12 (Cambridge: University Press, 1970), pp. 38, 58, *et passim*.

2 Filled with the Holy Spirit

There is much debate and often hard feelings and division over the meaning of being "filled with the Holy Spirit." In fact, there are a number of biblical expressions interchangeable with this one: "baptized in (or with) the Holy Spirit" and the coming of the Spirit in or upon someone. We shall see that these are various expressions for the same thing and that they apply to all God's people, not to a favored few.

Extent and Meaning

The expression "baptized in" or "baptized with" the Holy Spirit appears frequently in the New Testament. John the Baptist called his hearers to a water baptism based on repentance. It was an induction rite to outwardly signify one's turning from sin to God. John pointed to the Christ who would "baptize you in the Holy Spirit" (Mark 1:8). The parallels in Matthew 3:11 and Luke 3:16 add "and fire," the symbol of judgment or cleansing or both. Acts 1:5 repeats the promise that the followers of Jesus would be "baptized in (or with) the Holy Spirit."

John could point to the kingdom of God, God's coming as king to rule over men. John the Baptist was the proclaimer of the Spirit but not the bearer of the Spirit. But Jesus Christ was more than a messenger. He was uniquely the bearer of the Spirit. In him God not only spoke and acted but was uniquely present. Jesus not only pointed men to God; as Immanuel (God with us), he brought God to men.

The expression "the Holy Spirit shall come upon you" is another way of saying the same thing. The old explanation that there is a difference between the Spirit's coming *upon* and coming *in* is unbiblical and unsound. It is unwarranted to say that before Pentecost the Spirit came upon people and after Pentecost came within them, just as it is false to say that before Pentecost the Spirit came only temporarily but after Pentecost to abide.[1] This is exegetically unfounded and confusing. To come upon and to come within are only stylistic variations for the same thing. In fact, in Acts the term used is "upon" (1:8; 2:17), not "in" or "within," as the popular theory would require. Peter quoted Joel and applied it to the great outpouring of the Spirit on the day of Pentecost. The Spirit came *upon* the disciples, but surely in or within them. Theology here is *not* to be built upon the stylistic variation of prepositions.

Another false notion is that the Holy Spirit first came at Pentecost. Luke wrote two volumes, the Gospel bearing his name and the book of Acts, two volumes of the same continuing work. Luke describes John the Baptist as "filled with the Holy Spirit from his mother's womb" (Luke 1:15). Likewise, Elizabeth (Luke 1:41) and Zacharias were "filled with the Holy Spirit" (1:67). Of Simeon, a devout Jew, Luke says that the "Holy Spirit was upon him" (2:25) and that he came "in the Spirit into the temple" (2:27). This was before Pentecost, even before the birth of Jesus.

On the day of Pentecost, all the waiting disciples were "filled with the Holy Spirit" (Acts 2:4). But this very expression also describes John the Baptist, Elizabeth, Zacharias, Stephen, and Barnabas. Before as well as on and after Pentecost, God's people were filled with the Spirit. This filling was Pentecostal, but also pre-Pentecostal and post-Pentecostal. But more, we are told specifically how this filling of the Holy Spirit affected the lives and ministry of those so filled.

[1]Cf. R. B. Rackham, *The Acts of the Apostles*, "Westminster Commentaries" (London: Metheun & Co., 1939), p. 14, for this misconception.

John the Baptist was filled with the Spirit and he preached. He did not preach in ecstatic utterance, a "glossolalia" consisting of unintelligible utterance. He preached in plain language which all could understand. Filled with the Holy Spirit, he preached in language so plain that many ordinary people were converted. He preached so plainly that many of the religious leaders understood and felt threatened. He plainly called all to repentance. He plainly told those who had clothing and food to share with those who did not have. He told the tax collectors not to collect more than was due. He told the soldiers not to intimidate anyone (Luke 3:10-14). He preached in such plain language that the adultress Herodias had him beheaded (Matt. 14:1-12). John the Baptist was filled with the Holy Spirit, but he did not break out into unintelligible glossolalia. He preached the understood word of God. He sought no escape from the world in some mystical "tongue of angels," understandable only to God and the "spiritually elite." Filled with the Holy Spirit, he spoke plainly to the people before him, understandable to Sadducees, Pharisees, paganized rulers, and common people.

Zacharias was "filled with the Holy Spirit and he prophesied" (Luke 1:67). Luke gives the content of his prophesying. It was inspired preaching, intelligible preaching, not glossolalia. Zacharias quoted extensively from the Old Testament, telling of God's gracious promises and saving acts. He spoke plainly about God's covenant, his remembering his covenant, his deliverance of his people, enabling them to serve in holiness and righteousness. Zacharias was not a favored disciple at Pentecost. He was a Jewish priest, officiating at the Jewish Temple. He was filled with the Holy Spirit before Pentecost, before the birth of Jesus, and before the birth of John the Baptist. He was filled with the Holy Spirit and was thus empowered to worship God, to live in holiness and righteousness, and to preach the good news of redemption.

Stephen was a man "full of the Holy Spirit" (Acts 6:5). The first thing we learn about Stephen was that he was among the seven selected to care for the material needs of the poor. He was no other-worldly "enthusiast" caught up into the seventh heaven. He was "earthly" enough to be entrusted with the administering of money to meet daily needs of poor people. Next we learn that he preached, not in the unintelligible jargon of glossolalia but in plain, understandable words. In fact, he preached so plainly and with such penetrating insight into the Scriptures and the intention of God that many were so frustrated and threatened that they stoned him to death, Saul of Tarsus consenting to the deed.

Barnabas is another of whom it was said that he was "full of the Holy Spirit and faith" (Acts 11:24). The first thing that we learn of Barnabas is that he sold a farm and gave the whole price of it to the church for the feeding of the poor. This is true spirituality! This is one fruit of a Spirit-filled man! We learn also of Barnabas, this man who was "full of the Holy Spirit," that he risked his own reputation and life by standing up for Paul at a time when Paul was still suspect to the church in Jerusalem (Acts 9:27). He stood by Mark when Paul was determined to cast him aside (15:36-41). This same Mark whom Barnabas risked the ire of Paul to support, later wrote our earliest Gospel. Barnabas was "full of the Holy Spirit," and this moved him to share his material possessions, champion the "underdog," and give his life in missionary pioneering. Being "full of the Spirit" did not make Barnabas a sinless or perfect man. He faltered at Antioch when along with Peter he withdrew from table fellowship with uncircumcised brethren (Gal. 2:11-14). Being full of the Holy Spirit did not make Barnabas a sinless or perfect man, nor did it to our knowledge prompt him to "speak in tongues," but it did make him "a good man" in deed and word.

Being filled with the Holy Spirit is not the restricted or exclusive privilege of a favored few. It was not a second blessing, reserved for Pentecost or a select few in any age who see themselves standing in a Pentecostal line. Being filled with the Spirit did not lead to sinlessness. Barnabas is but one example of one who could be filled with the Spirit and yet fail as he did at Antioch, when in a moment of weakness he joined those who separated themselves from table fellowship which included some uncircumcised people (Gal. 2:11-14). Being filled with the Holy Spirit did not lead to unintelligible tongues and pride over assumed spiritual excellence. Those filled with the Holy Spirit gave themselves in humble, sacrificial service: food for the hungry, the gospel for the lost, support for those rejected. They were saints but yet sinners, being redeemed but not yet fully redeemed.

All Charismatic

All Christians are charismatic. The world has tried to take over this biblical concept. In the world, a person with "charisma" is one with sex appeal, social charm, political appeal, or the like. In the church today, charismatic people are thought to be those who move above the common herd into some higher, spiritual orbit. All such notions are false. In the New Testament, all God's people are saints (cf. 1 Cor. 1:1). All are being sanctified. All are "baptized" in or with the Spirit. The Spirit has come upon each. No one "possesses" the Holy Spirit, but the Holy Spirit possesses those who yield in humble faith. All Christians are charismatic.

Charismatic gifts are the gifts of God to us. All God's gifts are charismatic gifts. An instructive passage is Romans 12:6-8. Here Paul lists some of the gifts of God. "Charismatic" and "grace" are both built on the same Greek word (*charis*). Charismatic gifts are gifts of God's grace. They include prophecy (inspired preaching), ministry of all kinds, teaching, exhortation, distribution of material substance to the needy, and administration. One whose gift is that of charity or of administering any of the work of the church is a charismatic person!

What is a "charismatic movement" or a "charismatic revival"? These terms are much used today, but they are little informed by New Testament perspective or usage. The New Testament has much to say about the charismatic, but it has little resemblance to much of the ecstatic, otherworldly, and sometimes bizarre now associated with the "charismatic."

New Testament *charisma* is something from God but deeply rooted in history and in the world of flesh and blood. It is in keeping with the incarnation and not with flight from the realities of the world. When the Holy Spirit comes today it is not to take us out of the world but to give us a new kind of existence as we live responsibly in the world, precisely the burden of Jesus' prayer on the night before his crucifixion (cf. John 17:15). Jesus Christ brought to earth "the eternal life which was with the Father" (1 John 1:2), and in him it penetrated history and flesh so deeply and so tangibly that it could be "seen," "looked upon," and "handled" (1:1). It was "the Word of life" which in Jesus came into history and flesh so concretely that John could describe it as that which "we have heard, which we have seen with our eyes, which we have looked upon, and our hands have handled."

A movement or revival is not charismatic if it is moving in a direction opposite to the incarnation. The Holy Spirit does not come to undo the work of Jesus Christ or to reverse its direction. The Holy Spirit does not come to "unflesh" the Word. The Holy Spirit speaks and works as did Jesus Christ, in "enfleshed" words and deeds.

What is a "charismatic" revival or movement? It is one where the gifts of God are received and put to their intended service. It is a charismatic revival where one is moved by the Spirit of God to preach the gospel to sinners, feed the hungry, care for the sick, offer every man a place of dignity and meaning in the family of man. It is a charismatic revival wherever one puts his God-given talents or resources to the service of mankind: in the home, in the shop, in the store, in the office, in the school, in the pulpit, or wherever it is that the gifts of God are made to serve the needs of man.

"Charismatic revival" is not a banner to be seized by ecstatic enthusiasts gone into orbit. To the charismatic movement belong Zacharias, John the Baptist, Stephen, Philip, Barnabas, Paul, and all who minister in whatever capacity God has equipped them. If the one who writes these lines does so in the exercise of the "gifts" (*charismata*) he has from God, and if those who bring it to publication (publishers, editors, printers) do so in the exercise of their various "gifts" (*charismata*) which they have from God, we too belong to the "charismatic movement." The "charismatic movement" is as wide as are the people of God who are exercising their God-given abilities in the service of God, whether these services are spectacular, filling stadia and headlines, or unspectacular, possibly filling empty stomachs and empty lives.

The Fruit of the Spirit

The evidences of being "filled with the Spirit" are not all outward, although that is included. The ultimate tests are inward. The "fruit of the Spirit" is seen in terms of such primary qualities as "love, joy, peace, patience, kindness, goodness, faith (or faithfulness), gentleness, and self-control" (Gal. 5:22). It is not in sensational, flamboyant display but in those basic qualities of personal character and in serving the needs of mankind that one is found to be "filled with the Holy Spirit."

A closer look at Galatians 5:22 is highly instructive for understanding the character of one who is filled with the Spirit. Paul's key word is "fruit," a term made primary by Jesus himself. Jesus had taught that each person is to be known by his fruit (Matt. 7:15-23). It becomes clear from the context that Jesus did not confuse "fruit" with the outward matters of actions and words as such. Deeds and words may or may not reflect what one actually is. One with authentic existence under Christ will characteristically act and speak in accordance with what he is; but there is such a thing as sham or hypocrisy, and one can have all of the outward patterns of piety without ever knowing Christ. One may say "Lord, Lord!" and he may do mighty works and yet never have entered into a personal and saving knowledge of Christ (Matt. 7:22 f.). The "fruit," then, by which the true and false prophets or disciples are known may include words and deeds, but the fruit goes deeper than that.

In John 15:1-17 Jesus insisted upon two basic realities: (1) those abiding in him will produce what he meant by fruit, and (2) those not abiding in him cannot produce what he meant by fruit. Outward performance or show is possible with or without this abiding in him, but not so of "fruit." Man may of himself produce "results," words and deeds; but only from union with God, like the branch in the vine, can true fruit be produced. The nature or identity of this fruit is not described here, but love for one another seems best to be its fulfilment (15:8-17).

Paul comes nearest to spelling out what is meant by "fruit." He begins with love, that basic disposition in God and in those whom he transforms, the disposition to relate to others for their ultimate good, regardless of the cost to the one who so loves. Joy is more than the happiness which is affected by the constantly changing circumstances of life. Joy is the deep sense of fulfilment which enables one to celebrate the meaningfulness of life through all its changing circumstances. Jesus knew joy even as he faced the agony of the cross (Heb. 12:2). Peace is the *shalom* of God, total well-being for those committed to his care. Patience is the power to stand up under life's adversities. Kindness is the love which seeks the good of others. Goodness, too, belongs to the fruit of the Spirit. Scripture is not afraid to recognize goodness in man. A man's infinite capacity for evil is not denied, but neither is his infinite capacity for good under God. Man can be as evil as hate, greed, lust, murder, and rape. He can be good enough to turn the cheek when struck, to go the second mile in service that cannot be commanded, and to pray for his enemies. But goodness is not man's achievement. When man tries to be good, he botches it. Goodness appears only when the Spirit of God abides in a life. Faith and fidelity go together, and Paul's word *pistis* can mean either (cf. Rom. 3:3). Gentleness and a life under control round out his picture of the fruit of the Spirit. These are the qualities in human existence which best reflect that one is "filled with the Holy Spirit."

3   The Work of the Holy Spirit

Already we have observed that the Holy Spirit did not first come on the day of Pentecost. In the Old Testament and in the period covered by the Gospels the Spirit is as prominent as in Acts. Even Luke, who gives us the story of the outpouring of the Spirit on the day of Pentecost, begins his Gospel (Chap. 1-2) with what Barrett calls "*a pre-Christian* Church, equipped with the Holy Spirit and with prophets."[1] Elizabeth (1:41), Zacharias (1:67), and Simeon (2:25-27) were all filled with the Holy Spirit, and they prophesied. Likewise, John the Baptist was filled with the Holy Spirit, and he prophesied (1:15,17,76).

In an effort to understand the work of the Holy Spirit, we shall gather the biblical evidences around certain basic functions: the creative activity of God, prophecy, regeneration or renewal, exorcism, *paraklēsis*, missions, and nurture. In so doing, two acknowledgments are due: (1) this does not exhaust all that is attributed to the Holy Spirit and (2) the Scriptures do not themselves develop such a thematic structuring. This structuring attempts to meet our needs for understanding the work of the Spirit, derived hopefully from the Scriptures themselves.

The Creative Activity of God

Primal creation. The Spirit of God is mentioned as early as the second verse of Genesis (1:2). The very first claim of Genesis

[1] C. K. Barrett, *The Holy Spirit and the Gospel Tradition.* (New York: The Macmillan Co., 1947), p. 122.

is that God, in the beginning, created the heavens and the earth. Next we are told that "the earth was without form and void; and darkness was upon the face of the deep" (1:2). Against this background it is said that "the Spirit of God was moving over the face of the waters" (v.2). The creative work of God is here seen in terms of God's victory over chaos and darkness.[2] The idea of *creatio ex nihilo* (created out of nothing) is not excluded, but the emphasis is upon God's bringing order out of disorder (cosmos out of chaos) and light into darkness.[3]

There are two creation narratives in Genesis (1 to 2:4*a* and 2:4*b*-25). In the first narrative the earth is seen as a dark, watery chaos out of which is brought light and form. In the second narrative the earth is seen as a waterless waste which God made into a garden with vegetation and animals, and man over all.[4] In each narrative, creation is attributed to God directly and repeatedly. In 1:2 the creative activity is further ascribed to "the Spirit of God." It is not to be forgotten that in the New Testament the same creative activity of God is ascribed to "the Word" (John 1:1-5). Life and light in particular are ascribed to the Word (v. 4) as well as the overcoming of darkness by light (v. 5). This is strikingly reminiscent of the opening narrative of creation in Genesis. Of course, the Word was none other than Christ (1:14). Paul likewise attributes the divine creative activity to Christ: "In him were created all things in the heavens and upon the earth, things visible and things invisible, whether thrones or lordships or principalities or authorities; all things through him and unto him were created" (Col. 1:16).

Since creation is ascribed directly to God (Elohim in Gen. 1 to 2:4*a* and Yahweh in 2:4*b*-25), to the Spirit of God (Gen. 1:2),

[2]S. H. Hooke, "Genesis," *Peake's Commentary on the Bible* (London: Thomas Nelson and Sons, 1962), p. 179.

[3]Gerhard von Rad, *Genesis, a Commentary*, tr. by J. H. Mahs (2nd. ed. rev.; London: SCM Press, 1963), pp. 46 ff.

[4]Cf. Hooke, *op. cit.*, p. 179.

and to Christ (John 1:1-5),[5] it is highly precarious to interpret any one passage to the exclusion of the others. Surely, these and similar passages rule out any theology which sees divisions within God. Tritheism has no biblical support here. This should warn against any understanding of the Holy Spirit which sees the Spirit of God as distinct from God, as a fraction of God, or as the highest and most "spiritual" part of God. God is one God, in creation, revelation, and redemption—in everything and always. This by no means implies unitarianism, the denial of the deity of Jesus Christ; nor does it in any way deny the continuing presence of the Spirit of God. It does preclude any idea of polytheism (or tritheism) or division in God.

The birth of Jesus. Creation and procreation are different concepts, the former being much deeper rooted in Hebrew thought than the latter.[6] The idea of God's creative action permeates Scripture from first to last, but the idea of God procreating posed problems. Pagan myths were filled with stories of divine begettings, and from this Hebrew thought distinguished itself. Traces of the idea of divine begetting may be seen in passages like Psalm 2:7. However, the concept of divine begetting does emerge with force in the birth narrative of Jesus. He was seen not only to have been born of a virgin (Matt. 1:18,23; Luke 1:27), but to have been begotten of the Holy Spirit (Matt. 1:18,20; Luke 1:35). This was not the begetting of a new god; it was the begetting of the God-man.

The new creation. There probably is an intended parallel between the creative role of the Spirit of God in Genesis and certain New Testament statements. As the Spirit of God was the creative action of God in the primal creation, so now is the new creation begun in Jesus (cf. 2 Cor. 5:17). The older idea of divine creation remains the dominant one, but the newer idea of divine concep-

[5]These references are not exhaustive as to biblical evidence. See, e.g., Ps. 33:6 for "the word of the Lord" and Ps. 104:30 for God's "Spirit" as representing his creative action.

[6]Cf. Barrett, *op. cit.*, pp. 5-24.

tion comes in alongside. Both models, creation and begetting, are employed for the divine work of salvation. The "children of God" are ones "begotten of God" (John 1:13).[7] In John 3:5,6,8 the "Spirit" of whom one is to be begotten is presumably the Spirit of God.

That the idea of the new life as a divine begetting was not attributed to the Holy Spirit exclusively is reflected in Paul's claim, "In Christ Jesus through the gospel I begat you" (1 Cor. 4:15). In 1 John 2:29 the children of God are seen as begotten out of Christ, but elsewhere in this letter one is "begotten of God" (3:9; 4:7; 5:1,4,18). Again we should be warned against making too much of distinctions between the Father, the Son, and the Holy Spirit. The identical function is ascribed to each. We do not have three gods, and neither is God divided up into three parts. The Holy Spirit is the Spirit of *God*, and Jesus Christ is *God* with us (Immanuel).

The Spirit and Prophecy

In his sermon in Jerusalem on the day of Pentecost, Peter quoted Joel 2:28-32, claiming the fulfilment of God's promise through Joel that "in the last days" God would pour out from his Spirit and sons and daughters would prophesy (Acts 2:17-18). The giving of the Holy Spirit on that occasion had as one of its chief manifestations the inspired preaching (prophecy) which followed. The "tongues" in which the followers of Christ spoke articulated the promises of God and his call to repentance. These "tongues" were intelligible and powerful, bringing thousands into new life and a new fellowship.

Next to the creative activity of God, the Spirit of God was known as the Spirit of prophecy. In the Old Testament there is a close relationship between prophecy and the Holy Spirit. Zechariah condemns the adamant hearts of those who turned

[7]Some Old Latin manuscripts and a number of early church fathers, including Irenaeus, Tertullian, and Origen, have the singular "who" rather than the plural, relating the begetting to Jesus rather than to his followers.

deaf ears to "the law and the words which the Lord of hosts had sent by his Spirit through the former prophets" (7:12). Stephen's heaviest indictment was upon those who "resist the Holy Spirit," as was true of his tormentors and their fathers in former generations (Acts 7:51).

The "unpardonable sin" has to do with deliberate rejection of the revelatory work of the Holy Spirit (Matt. 12:22-32; Mark 3:20-30; Luke 11:14-23; 12:10). To look upon the obvious work of the Holy Spirit and call it the work of Beelzebul is inexcusable. Jesus could forgive any affront to his own person, but to wilfully close one's eyes to the obvious work of the Holy Spirit is inexcusable now and for all time (Matt. 12:31 f.). Jesus had just healed a man who had been both blind and deaf (12:22). To Jesus, this was clear evidence of "the Spirit of God" and of the arrival of the kingdom of God (12:28). The healing power of God's Spirit was also a revealing power, scorned only by minds closed to truth and light. Barrett puts it succinctly, "The Holy Spirit is the Spirit of prophecy; all the prophets spoke by the Holy Spirit."[8] Jesus recognized that David was inspired by the Holy Spirit as he spoke of God's overcoming work (Mark 12:36). When Elizabeth, Zachariah, Simeon, and John the Baptist were filled with the Holy Spirit, they prophesied (Luke 1:15,35,41,67; 2:25). Prophecy sometimes was a foretelling of the future, and always it was telling forth the word of God to the people in the prophet's presence.

Although the Spirit of God stands for God's revealing activity, again we are warned against pressing too far any distinctions within God. It is to be remembered that "Thus sayeth the Lord" is an Old Testament refrain. God has always done his own talking. Then, too, Jesus Christ is "the Word" of God. He is "the Light" as well as "the Life." No part of the Gospel tradition is more certainly the words of Jesus himself than the antitheses in the Sermon on the Mount: "Ye have heard it said . . . , but I say unto you . . ." (Matt. 5:21f.,27f.,31f.,33f.,38f.,43f.). God speaks;

[8]*Op. cit.*, p. 108.

the Spirit of God speaks; Jesus Christ speaks—and it is all one divine action. This is quite emphatic in the seven letters in the Revelation, where the same words are attributed to Christ and the Spirit (Rev. 2—3). The words are those of Christ (2:1,8,12, 18; 3:1,7,14). The same words are "what the Spirit says to the churches" (Rev. 2:7,11,17,29; 3:6,13,22). The overriding point here is that God is one God, and he is a speaking God. Revelation is God's self-disclosure to his people.[9]

Exorcism and Kingdom

"The Lord is the Spirit; and where the Spirit of the Lord is, there is freedom" (2 Cor. 3:17). In this context, Paul had in mind primarily our freedom from the Mosaic law in the new covenant of God's grace, but the truth is more embracing than that. Paul goes on to speak of the dynamic change which ultimately brings man to fulfilment, to God's intended glory for man. All of this comes from "the Lord who is the Spirit" (v. 18).

"The Lord" may refer to God or to Christ. Paul's basic monotheism enabled him to move easily from reference to God, to Christ, and to the Spirit. This is striking in Romans 8:9-10, where Paul speaks of "the Spirit of God," "the Spirit of Christ," and "Christ" with no apparent change of subject. Christ means freedom: "If the Son shall set you free, ye shall be free indeed" (John 8:36). The Holy Spirit means freedom, for "where the Spirit of the Lord is there is freedom" (2 Cor. 3:17). The Spirit of God means freedom, for God is a liberating God.

Exorcism. The Gospels have many stories of exorcism, the freeing of someone from a "demon."[10] These "demon possessed" people are described in various states of physical illness and impairment as well as emotional and mental disorder. Some showed

---

[9]See John Baillie, *The Idea of Revelation in Recent Thought* (New York: Columbia University Press, 1956), p. 47.

[10]For a cogent discussion of the distinction between the demonic and satanic, see Ragnar Leivestad, *Christ the Conqueror* (New York: Macmillan, 1954).

signs of suicidal mania. All were broken, lonely, and rejected. The "demons" immediately recognized Jesus as their enemy; he had come to destroy them (Mark 1:24). Jesus did exactly that. Wherever he was able to win over the trust of one of those disturbed people, he freed him of his guilt, phobias, schizophrenia, or whatever else it was that had alienated him from God, from other people, and from his own true identity (Mark 5:15).

For anyone today who can go through a single day without thinking about demons, the demons have been destroyed. Few people today, if any, live with the fear of demons known to many in Jesus' day. For example, we may fear to drink untested water because of the possibility of germs or impurities, but few would fear thus to drink a demon. Many protest strip-mining because of ecological damage, but we hear no warnings that we may thus disturb some resident demon and incur his wrath. And, fortunately, we increasingly offer medical help to physically ill and mentally or emotionally disturbed people and increasingly frown upon cursing, banning, beating, burning, or jailing such victims, as was done before Jesus came "to destroy the demons."

Exorcisms in the Gospels, especially Mark, are a primary witness to the inbreaking of the kingdom of God in the person of Christ. This is the bold claim made by Jesus in reply to his opponents who charged him with drawing upon the power of Beelzebul: "If by the finger of God I cast out demons, then indeed the kingdom of God has arrived" (Luke 11:20). Matthew has "Spirit of God" (12:28). Luke's "finger of God" is no doubt more primitive, an Old Testament idiom for the activity of God. In all three Synoptics the overcoming of "demons" is seen as a major sign that God's sovereign rule, his kingdom, is uniquely present in Jesus and is overcoming the kingdom of evil, foreshadowing an even greater victory to come.

Overcoming the demonic is one work of the Holy Spirit. To state it another way, the Spirit of God is God's mighty action in overcoming the demonic. But this is likewise Christ's work (Mark 1:24), and it is nothing less than the overcoming kingship of God

(Luke 11:20).

The temptations of Jesus. It may seem incongruous to follow a discussion of exorcisms with the temptations of Jesus, but there is some connection as well as significant dissimilarity. Jesus had in no sense suffered the alienation or impairments of the "demoniacs," but he did do battle within himself with some of the very forces from which he delivered the demoniacs. Mark has a very terse account of Jesus' wilderness temptations (1:12-13). Into his two verses he packs a number of ingredients: (1) The Spirit it was who "thrust him into the wilderness"; (2) it was a deserted place, such as characterized demons, into which Jesus was cast; (3) and Jesus was tempted by Satan. Matthew (4:1-11) and Luke (4:1-13) have fuller accounts, with descriptions of the temptations. All three Synoptics agree that Jesus was tempted by Satan (Mark) or the devil (Matthew and Luke), yet each in some way relates the temptations to the Holy Spirit. It was by the Spirit that Jesus was moved into this agony.

It must be noted that in none of the Synoptic Gospels are demons mentioned in connection with the wilderness temptations of Jesus. Mark may have a hint as to demons in his reference to a deserted place, a common habitation of demons, but this is not explicit."[11] Both Matthew and Luke are explicit that it was by "the devil" that Jesus was tempted (Matt. 4:1; Luke 4:2). This is in keeping with the New Testament distinction between "demons" and "the devil" or "Satan." In the New Testament, "demoniacs" are people to be pitied, more victimized than guilty. In the New Testament "Satan" or "the devil" always implies the guilt of the one into whom Satan "enters," as with Judas (John 13:27). When Peter resisted Jesus' statements about his role of suffering, Jesus said, "Get behind me, Satan" (Matt. 16:23). Jesus was not exonerating Peter but condemning him as guilty. Whatever else is implied, the New Testament employment of the term "Satan" is to stress human responsibility and guilt. Employment

---

[11]Barrett, *op. cit.*, p. 49, citing Strack-Billerbeck, *Kommentar*, IV. 516 d.

of the term "demons" implies a pitiful state of bondage, brokenness, or alienation calling for loving care.

The Synoptics see Jesus to have entered into temptation and to have prevailed over "the devil" as he was led by and empowered by the Holy Spirit. Jesus' temptations were real. They were not sham battles. They were not straw men which he overcame. Something within Jesus was drawn toward means and goals which he rejected. There were options before him and he struggled with these options. Temptation is not of itself sin, and Jesus did not sin. He did have to struggle through options as to what he would undertake to do and how he would achieve his mission. The wilderness temptations related specifically to his mission.

Jesus rejected the messianic hopes and ideals of his people. They longed for a messianic deliverance from Roman rule. They longed for a restored Israel. Jesus did care about his people. He did want the hungry to be fed and the captives to be freed. But he rejected brute force as the means, and he rejected a nationalistic understanding of the kingdom of God. He would give himself to the kingdom of God, but it would be a kingdom embracing all men and not just one nation. He would establish God's righteous rule not with a sword but a cross, not by taking life but by giving it. Led and empowered by the Spirit of God, Jesus did overcome "Satan" in these wilderness temptations. This was not "exorcism," a victory over "demons"; but it was a victory over Satan.

The Paraclete and Paraclesis

The term "paraclete" is much more restricted in the New Testament than "Spirit," "Holy Spirit," "the Spirit of God," and like expressions. The term seems to have various usages, but it is one term employed in the New Testament by which to set forth certain aspects of the work of the Holy Spirit.

The term "paraclete" appears only in John 14:16,26; 15:26; 16:7; and 1 John 2:1. In John 14:26 the paraclete is "the Spirit of truth." In 1 John 2:1 Jesus Christ is himself the paraclete. John 14:16 is ambiguous, for it could read: "Another paraclete," implying that Jesus is a paraclete and so is the other, or "another, a paraclete," implying that only the Holy Spirit is the paraclete. Again, the warning flags go up against tritheism or any actual partitioning of God. In the New Testament *paraclesis* (a cognate form of *paraclete*) is God's work (Rom. 15:5; 2 Cor. 1:3); the Holy Spirit is the Paraclete; and Jesus Christ is the Paraclete.

The cognates paraclete and paraclesis are derived from the Greek preposition *para* (alongside) and *kalein* (to call). Literally, the paraclete is one called to the side of another. But etymology does not represent the full force of a word, only its point of origin. In the New Testament various ministries are attributed to the paraclete or to the *paraklesis* of God. These include comfort, defense, guidance, teaching, and conviction.

A major work of the Spirit has to do with truth and the teaching of the truth. The Spirit is sometimes termed "the Spirit of Truth" (John 14:17; 15:26; 16:13). The truth which the Spirit communicates is the truth that was embodied in Jesus Christ, the one who said, "I am the way, the truth, and the life" (14:6). The Spirit's work of teaching the truth is an extension of the work of Jesus as both embodiment and teacher of the truth. The Spirit will remind Jesus' followers of the things Jesus taught (14:26). He will guide into all truth, again the truth Jesus embodied and taught. In this continuing work of the Spirit, the further implications and applications of the truth of Jesus Christ is brought out.

A part of the work of the Spirit is that of judgment. He will convict the world of sin, of righteousness, and of judgment (16:8-11). The basic sin is that of failure to trust the reality of God as it confronts us in Jesus Christ. The Spirit will also vindicate Jesus as righteous, showing that though he was rejected and crucified he has been vindicated as righteous in his resurrection and enthronement, in that he "goes to the Father." The Spirit will show that the triumphant way of Jesus Christ is the exposure and judgment of "the prince of this world."

The Holy Spirit has the further role of advocate. He stands by the people of God in their times of trial. Jesus encouraged his followers to boldly live their lives and give their witness without fear of the consequences, assuring them that if brought to trial the Holy Spirit would be there to speak through them and in their behalf (Mark 13:11). This passage has often been misinterpreted and misapplied to relate to pulpit sermons, as though reliance upon the Holy Spirit is a proper substitute for study and preparation of sermons. The promise is not for that but for one brought to trial because of his faithful witness. It is to assure us that God will not forsake his faithful witness.

A further work of the Paraclete is to stand by the followers of Christ when they sin (1 John 2:1). The ideal is that they not sin at all, but true followers are yet subject to temptation and sin. When they do sin, they have a Paraclete, here understood as an advocate, one who pleads their cause for them. The English word "advocate" (from Latin) is the equivalent of the word "paraclete" (from Greek). Etymologically, each word pictures one as called alongside. The functions are many, here to plead one's cause; but the idea of the continuing divine presence is behind all New Testament usages of the term Paraclete.

The term "paraclete" affirms the continuing divine presence, beyond the historical life of Jesus of Nazareth. It also cautions us against tritheism. In John 14:26 the Paraclete is explicitly identified with the Holy Spirit. In 1 John 2:1 the Paraclete is explicitly identified with "Jesus Christ the righteous one." Some scholars see this as evidence that different authors wrote the Gospel of John and the First Epistle of John.[12] That may be true, but it is far from established. It is more likely that the writer's theology and his understanding of God permitted him to apply the term Paraclete equally to the Holy Spirit and to Jesus Christ who continues to be our advocate. To John, as to Paul, the risen Christ and the Holy Spirit represent the same divine presence.

---

[12]Cf. C. H. Dodd, *The Johannine Epistles*, "Moffatt New Testament Commentary" (New York: Harper & Brothers, 1946), pp. xlvii-lvi.

Missions

Whatever else may be said of the book of Acts, it gives major attention to the thrust of the gospel into various communities of people in the world: Jews, Samaritans, God-fearing Gentiles already attracted to Judaism, and pagans clearly outside the reach of Judaism.[13] Luke's term for this divine impulse behind this missionary thrust into not only ever-widening geographical areas but more importantly across the barriers of nationality, race, and ritual differences is often but not exclusively "The Holy Spirit." His overriding concern seemed to be to trace the movement of the gospel from the heart of pietistic Judaism (Luke 1-2) to the heart of the Graeco-Roman world (Acts 28:31), ascribing this missionary thrust to none other than God himself. The very divine presence encountered in "all that Jesus began to do and to teach" (Acts 1:1) is the same divine presence which as "the Holy Spirit" empowered them for witness "unto the end of the earth" (1:8).

That terminology was fluid and the oneness of God was uncompromised is apparent from the narrative of the sending of Philip on mission to the eunuch of Ethiopia and on to Azotus and Caesarea (8:26-40). In 8:26 it was "an angel of the Lord" who spoke to Philip, sending him on a mission toward Gaza, where he met the eunuch. Next it was "the Spirit" who told Philip to "be joined to this chariot" (8:29). Then it was by "the Spirit of the Lord" (8:39) that Philip was "snatched away" and sent by way of Azotus to Caesarea to evangelize the area. "An angel of the Lord," "the Spirit," and "the Spirit of the Lord" seem to be interchangeable terms for the same divine presence. Here the Spirit's work is seen in terms of evangelism or missions.

Both conversion and commission may be traced as readily to the risen Christ as to the Spirit. It was "the Lord," identified as "Jesus" (Acts 9:5) who appeared to Saul of Tarsus and brought

[13]Cf. the unfolding of this theme in my commentary, *The Book of Acts: The Early Struggle for an Unhindered Gospel* (Nashville: Broadman Press, 1955), *passim*.

him under conviction and to faith. It was "the Lord" who sent Ananias to Saul in Damascus (9:10 f.) to give him guidance, and presumably "the Lord" here is Jesus (9:13). It was "the Lord," presumably Jesus, who commissioned Saul to bear his name "before Gentiles and kings and sons of Israel" (9:15). The book of Acts is thus able to ascribe the identical work to the risen Jesus or to the Spirit. Saul was promised the recovery of his sight and that he would be "filled with the Holy Spirit" (9:17), but already the very power elsewhere attributed to the Spirit (conviction, conversion, commission) came to him in terms of the Lord Jesus.

Frequent interchanges of terms appear in Acts 10-11, in the story of Peter and Cornelius. An "angel of God" appeared to Cornelius (10:3), whom Cornelius could address (10:4) as "sir" (*kyrios*) or refer to as "a man" (10:30). The "voice" which addressed Peter is addressed by Peter as "Lord" (10:13-15), yet this very commission to go to the house of Cornelius is attributed to "the Spirit" (10:19; 11:12). Finally, the whole mission to Cornelius and its results are attributed to "God," whose directive was not to be opposed (11:17). The missionary thrust, here sending the reluctant apostle across the racial lines separating Jew from Gentile, was that of God, whether described in terms of an "angel of the Lord," the "Lord," or the "Spirit." This was the same divine presence "angel, Spirit, Spirit of the Lord" as had sent Philip joyfully across the lines separating Jew from Samaritan or Jew from an Ethiopian eunuch.

The most ambitious missions described in Acts begin with a mighty impulse and outward thrust from Antioch of Syria, attributed to "the Holy Spirit" (13:2,4). Under this impulse distant lands are reached, but more importantly stubborn lines dividing Jew from Gentile are crossed. This chiefly is the story Luke tells. A major message of Acts is that such crossing of lines of prejudice is the work of the Holy Spirit. The Spirit of God is on the side of the unity of the whole human race under the lordship of Christ, not on the side of prejudice, division, and bigotry. Missions is a major work of the Spirit of God, not only to all men but to all men as equally precious, with no place for the old, worldly fragmenting lines.

Nurture

Attention has been given already to "the fruit of the Spirit" (Chap. 2). This ground need not be retraced here, but it is to be made emphatic that the work of the Spirit includes that of Christian nurture. There is no surer evidence that the Spirit is at work in a life than "the fruit" produced by the Spirit (Gal. 5:22). Creeds can be recited, ritual acts performed, and behavioral patterns exhibited with or without God's Spirit. But such qualities as love, joy, peace, patience, kindness, goodness, faith, fidelity, gentleness, and self-control come only from the Spirit of God, and where the Spirit of God is at work they will appear.

4   The Holy Spirit and Tongues

Glossolalia or tongue speaking is a subject unknown in the New Testament outside the book of Acts and First Corinthians. Mark 16:17 is not found in our oldest and most dependable manuscripts and is considered spurious by almost all scholars.[1] We read of "other tongues" and "tongues" in Acts 2:4; 10:46; and 19:6. Chapters 12—14 of First Corinthians deal chiefly with a form of tongues in Corinth, a form less like than like the phenomenon at Pentecost (Acts 2). There is no Greek term in the New Testament for "unknown" tongues.

Tongues at Pentecost

Luke reports an amazing occurrence in Jerusalem at the Feast of Pentecost following the death and resurrection of Jesus.

Source theories. Some modern exponents of glossolalia try to discredit the idea that the tongues at Pentecost were intelligible. They do so by appeal to source criticism, contending that Luke has overlaid an older tradition of unintelligible, ecstatic utterance with a later tradition that the speech at Pentecost was intelligible.

---

[1]Almost all scholars agree that the authentic text of Mark ends with 16:8, but they are not agreed as to whether this was the original ending or the original ending was lost. A variety of endings beyond 16:8 appear in extant manuscripts. The most reliable manuscripts in Greek, Latin, and Syriac, as well as later versions and early church fathers agree in concluding with 16:8. The ending consisting of 16:9-20 is traceable from the latter half of the second century until its triumph in the popular texts of the fourth century onward.

By this reconstruction through source analysis, the claim is made that the Corinthian model is the older, corresponding to the tradition Luke has buried under a later version. Those approaching the matter thus appeal to the charge that those speaking in "other tongues" were "drunk with new wine" (Acts 2:13). They hold that this reflects the older layer, the newer one being represented by Luke's claim that each of the pilgrims understood in his own dialect (2:8).

Source criticism is a valid and often a rewarding method in biblical study. That Luke had oral and written sources before him is made explicit in the preface to his two volumes (Luke 1:1-4). Not only does he seem to employ sources in the Gospel but also in Acts. But the application of source criticism to the event on the day of Pentecost does not yield the results claimed for it by its champions.

There is nothing new about the claim that the early chapters of Acts are composed of at least two sources.[2] In fact there are many theories, with little agreement as to the reconstruction of these alleged sources. One of the latest attempts on the part of critical scholarship to isolate Luke's sources behind Acts 1—5 yields the following results: Source A represented by 1:12-14; 3:1-10; 4:1 to 5:12a and Source B represented by 1:1-11; 1:15 to 2:47; 3:11-26; 5:12b-42, Source A being considered the older.[3] According to this theory, Acts did not originally contain 1:1-11; 1:15-2:47; 3:11-26; 5:12b-42, this being a later addition from an inferior source. This is only one of many source analyses, dating back to B. L. Koningsmann's proposal in 1798 that the author of

[2]Cf. Frank Stagg, E. Glenn Hinson, and Wayne E. Oates, *Glossolalia: Tongue Speaking in Biblical, Historical, and Psychological Perspective* (Nashville: Abingdon Press, 1967), pp. 29-31, for a fuller analysis of this point and for the whole issue of glossolalia. This present chapter does not displace the book published with two of my colleagues, for that book covers a far wider area relating to tongues. Likewise, this present book, although it overlaps with respect to glossolalia, is concerned with a subject more inclusive than glossolalia.

[3]A. Q. Morton and G. H. C. MacGregor, *The Structure of Luke and Acts* (New York: Harper & Row, 1965), pp. 36, 44.

Acts was to be distinguished from the author of the "we passages" in Acts and including Adolf Harnack's theory that Acts 3:1 to 5:16 belongs to what he termed "Recension A" and that chapters 2—3 and 5:17-42 represent a late and almost worthless "Recension B."[4]

According to Morton and MacGregor, Acts 4:31 is the earliest description of what occurred in Jerusalem on the day of Pentecost: "And when they prayed, the place in which they were gathered was shaken; and they were all filled with the Holy Spirit and spoke the word of God with all boldness." This text is acknowledged by all scholars as primary, and it connects normal speech with the coming of the Holy Spirit.

Source theories for Acts 1—5 are highly precarious, as is reflected in the wide divergences among those who travel this way. It is not our purpose here to assess source theories as such. What we would recognize here is that one cannot on the basis of any source theory yet advanced by serious scholarship eliminate from Acts the view that "tongues" at Pentecost represented intelligible speech. If anything by source analysis is to be eliminated as secondary, it would work the other way. By all source theories it is precisely Chapter 2 which suffers most. I am far from accepting these source theories as they now stand, but even if for argument's sake they should be granted, tongues at Pentecost remain intelligible. One cannot have it both ways, by source criticism rejecting Luke's version of intelligible speech but at the same time retaining matters which the same source theories would reject: the outpouring of the Holy Spirit, Peter's sermon, three thousand conversions, and beautiful *koinonia*, all of which belong to the alleged secondary source. The evidences compel the conclusion, whether one follows source theories or not, that Luke's representation of tongues at Pentecost as intelligible speech is primary and not to be set aside.

The story and its meaning. Whether Luke employed sources or not, Chapter 2 belongs to Acts as it has reached us, and it is

[4]See *Ibid.*, p. 103, fn. 11 for details.

proper to try to understand it as it stands. In Acts 2 the gift of tongues is seen as a miracle of some sort, whether of speech or hearing or both. Jewish pilgrims had gathered in Jerusalem, having come from many countries with their different linguistic backgrounds. What amazed them was that each was able to understand in the language or dialect of his birth (2:8). Luke stresses the fact of understanding without explaining how this was possible. To explain it on naturalistic grounds, for example that various languages were spoken, is not what Luke seems to imply. He seems to indicate that it was the gift of the Holy Spirit and not the linguistic competence of the people that made understanding possible on this occasion. The amazement of the people would not be simply that they found numerous languages being spoken, for that was a common experience then as now in the Middle East.

However baffling to us as to those who were there, Luke intends to represent a miracle. With the gift of the Holy Spirit there were certain audio and visual signs *like* a mighty, rushing wind and tongues of fire. It was the Holy Spirit who "gave them utterance" as they "began to speak in other tongues" (2:1-4). Peter rejected as unfounded the charge of drunkenness and identified the experience as fulfilment of the promise found in the prophet Joel, who predicted the outpouring of the Spirit in the last days, accomplished by prophesy (inspired preaching), as well as the seeing of visions and dreaming of dreams, accompanied by signs from heaven (2:15 ff.). Peter interpreted this in terms of evangelistic, inspired preaching designed to lead men to call upon God that they might be saved (2:17-21). This does not imply what Behm termed "a mass ecstasy on the part of the disciples which includes outbreaks of glossolalia."[5]

Luke uses "tongues" and "dialects" as equivalents (2:4,8), and he uses "dialects" for known languages (1:19; 2:6,8). In 1:19 "dialect" refers to the Aramaic word *akeldema*, "field of blood."

[5]Johannes Behm, "Tongues, Other Tongues," *Theological Dictionary of the New Testament* (Grand Rapids: Wm. B. Eerdmans, 1964), Vol. I, p. 721.

In 2:6,8 each is said to have heard the "tongues" in his own "dialect," that is, language. The same utterance is termed "other tongues" in 2:11. The identical Greek term is used in 2:4, where the Holy Spirit gave "utterance" *(apophtheggesthai)* to those who began "to speak in other tongues" and in 2:14, where "Peter with the eleven lifted up his voice and gave utterance (*apephthegsato*) to them." This "utterance" (tongues, dialect) was inspired, understandable preaching. Joel had called it "prophesying," and it is this interpretation which Peter gives to the "tongues" which scoffers attributed to drunkenness but Peter attributed to the Holy Spirit. Clearly, in Acts 2 "tongues" relates to prophecy, not Corinthian-like ecstasy.

Luke's real emphasis in Acts 2 is upon the gift of the Holy Spirit, only secondarily upon "tongues." This parallels his emphasis in the early chapters of his Gospel. Just as he traces the birth and mission of Jesus to the Holy Spirit (Luke 1:15,35,41,67; 2:26; 3:22), so does he trace the birth or empowering of the church for its mission to the Holy Spirit.[6] One may speculate that Luke's further purpose was to draw a parallel between the giving of the gospel at Pentecost with the giving of the law at Sinai, the reversal of the confusion of tongues at Babel, or the new creation at Pentecost as a parallel to God's initial work of creation as seen in Genesis, where "the Spirit brooded over the waters."[7] These theories are possible and significant but uncertain. What does emerge with force is that Luke's emphasis is upon the Holy Spirit, not primarily upon the unique and passing means given for this great epoch in Christian history. "Tongues" in the Pentecostal pattern stopped; the Spirit remains.

Traits at Pentecost. More important than the outward signs

[6]Cf. R. R. Williams, *The Acts of the Apostles*, "The Torch Bible Commentaries" (London: SCM Press, 1953), p. 39.

[7]For these theories see Kirsopp Lake, "The Gift of the Spirit on the Day of Pentecost," *The Beginnings of Christianity*, ed. F. J. Foakes-Jackson and Kirsopp Lake (London: Macmillan, 1933), V, 112-14; and Ernst Haenchen, *The Acts of the Apostles*, 14th ed. tr. by B. Noble, G. Shinn, R. McL. Wilson (Philadelphia: Westminster Press, 1971), pp. 166-75.

and temporary means employed at Pentecost is the abiding presence of the Holy Spirit and the salutory effects upon the church. The Spirit empowered them, united them, and gave them a beautiful fellowship in worship, preaching, teaching, sharing, and joy! They continued to give themselves "to the teaching of the apostles, and to fellowship (*koinonia*), and to the breaking of bread, and to prayer" (2:42).

Koinonia is a prominent term for describing the church upon whom the Holy Spirit came at Pentecost. *Koinonia* means the "common life" shared with the Father and his Son and with one another (1 John 1:1-3). This koinonia included the sharing of their material substance with one another (2:44-46; 4:32-37). No one looked upon his property as really his own. It was all the gift of God to be viewed as a sacred trust, to be made available to each as he had need. Barnabas, a man full of the Spirit, exemplified the spirit of the group when he sold a field and turned over the full price for the care of the needy. Thousands were brought to repentance and a new kind of life. They met daily in the praise of God and the enjoyment of a common meal. These are the real marks of a people upon whom the Holy Spirit is poured. These are the marks of those "baptized with the Spirit" or "filled with the Spirit."

Tongues at Caesarea and Ephesus

Twice only outside Chapter 2 are tongues mentioned in Acts, receiving bare mention in 10:46 and 19:6. In each case the primary emphasis is upon the Holy Spirit, the gift of tongues being one manifestation of the Spirit's presence. It may be significant that Luke's three references to the gift of tongues fall at important junctures in the progress of the gospel, to the Jews in Jerusalem at Pentecost (Chap. 2), to the Gentile household of Cornelius at Caesarea (Chap. 10), and to followers of John the Baptist in Ephesus who needed to go on to Jesus Christ (Chap. 19).

The precise nature of tongues at Caesarea and Ephesus is not clear, whether like the understandable tongues at Pentecost or the unintelligible tongues in Corinth. There was no apparent language barrier in Caesarea and Ephesus as was true in Jerusalem, so there was no apparent need for a miracle of communication as in Jerusalem. This would argue for some parallel to Corinth rather than Jerusalem, but this is not demonstrable either way.

Luke reports that those at Caesarea were heard "speaking in tongues and extolling God" (10:46), and those in Ephesus "were speaking in tongues and were prophesying" (19:6). At least "extolling" God seems to imply intelligible speech in Acts 2:17 f.; and in 1 Corinthians 14 prophecy is distinguished from tongues, the former being intelligible, the latter not. The phenomena at Caesarea and Ephesus could correspond to that at Corinth or represent a halfway step between tongues at Jerusalem and Corinth. What is clear is the sharp distinction between tongues at Pentecost and Corinth.

Tongues in Corinth

Apart from Acts, the phenomenon of "tongues" is known to the New Testament only in 1 Corinthians 12—14. Apart from a spurious ending to Mark (see above), the Gospels are silent on the subject. If "tongues" is the ultimate gift of the Spirit, it is strange that Jesus, the bearer of the Spirit, was without the gift! Not only are tongues not attributed to Jesus, but he scorned "babbling" along with "much speaking" as pagan and not proper to the people of God (Matt. 6:7). He was sometimes silent (Matt. 27:14; Mark 15:4 f.; Luke 23:9; John 19:9 f.), but never did he break out into unintelligible utterance. He "groaned" at the grave of Lazarus (John 11:33), but this was not glossolalia. This was an inarticulate expression of deep emotion, a universal human experience under stress. When Jesus spoke, it was in the language of the people before him, direct and simple in statement and profound in meaning—as straightforward as the Beatitudes, the antitheses, and the parables.

It is remarkable that of all Paul's letters, only in 1 Corinthians is there any trace of glossolalia. Paul made much of the Holy Spirit but little of tongues. Romans, for example, gives major attention to the Holy Spirit (5:5; 7:6; 8:2, 6-14,26-28; 14:17) but never mentions tongues. Galatians has instructions for those who are "spiritual" (6:1) and describes "the fruit of the Spirit" (5:22) but says nothing about "tongues."

Why Corinth? There is no conclusive answer to the question as to why it is only in Corinth that the problem of glossolalia enters into Paul's discussions. The question is a proper one, however elusive the answer. It is difficult to resist the suggestion that the ultra-pagan nature of Corinth had something to do with it. Paul worked in and wrote to other pagan cities, but none more pagan than Corinth.

There was a history of religious ecstasy in Greece and its neighboring lands, sometimes quite excessive. Orphism, for example, was characterized by such expression before the time of Plato. Drawing upon the Thracian worship of Dionysus, Orphism offered a new understanding of man as a dualism of immortal soul and a body, the soul being a divine creation with greater freedom and fulfilment outside the body than within it. The Thracians conducted torchlight festivals in the night on mountaintops or slopes, marked by loud instrumental music, wild dancing, and shrill crying. Frantic whirling in circular dances continued until the dancers, mostly women, carrying snakes sacred to their god, finally attained to a sacred frenzy and then fell upon some beast selected as their victim and devoured it.[8] In this experience of "sacred madness" the "soul" seemed to leave the body and enter into union with God (*entheos*). This union with their god was their "enthusiasm" (*entheos*) or god-intoxication. Esctasy *(ekstasis)* is a "standing outside" of oneself. This escape into freedom of the "soul" from the body was the chief goal of the cult. They wanted to be "unfleshed," not incarnate.

Scholars are in near full agreement that the church in Corinth

[8]Erwin Rohde, *Psyche*, tr. W. B. Willis from 8th German ed. (New York: Harcourt, Brace & Co., 1925), p. 257.

was marked by "enthusiasm," whatever its origin or precise nature. Some see gnosticism as already having emerged there.[9] Others are more cautious, holding that the origins of gnosticism are yet obscure, whether pre-Christian or not, whether having derived from Judaism, paganism, or Christianity.[10] What is clearest is that there were at least gnosticizing tendencies in Corinth, with great value placed upon "enthusiasm." What was prized was a "spirituality" which give "freedom," sometimes interpreted as sexual license (5:1 f.), and which rejected the idea of the resurrection of the body in favor of the freedom of the "immortal soul" from the body (Chap. 15).

Not only are there striking parallels between the enthusiasm at Corinth and some features of Orphism, but in Judaism itself there are traces of such concern for ecstasy. Among the early Hebrew prophets appeared "the professionalized *nebi'im* who, as Jahweh enthusiasts, wandered about the country in bands, working themselves into religious frenzy by means of music and dancing (1 Sam. 10:5-13; 19:18-24; 2 Sam. 6:13-17; 1 Kings 20:35-37)."[11] It may have been because of these excesses that men like Amos disclaimed any identity with the *nebi'im* (Amos 7:14). Probably the notion that the true self is a nonmaterial "soul" which longs for its freedom from the body arose in various religious groups. It could grow out of the experience of dreams, where the person asleep seems released from the limits of the body to roam the earth freely. In any case, ecstasy (standing outside the body) and enthusiasm (union with deity) are ancient and widespread concerns of various religions. "Tongues" is one example of ecstatic escape, and it was probably thought of as a divine lan-

[9]See Walter Schmithals, *Gnosticism in Corinth*, tr. John E. Steely (Nashville: Abingdon Press, 1971), who is a strong advocate for the view that gnosticism was the major problem at Corinth and in other Pauline churches.

[10]See R. McL. Wilson, *Gnosis and the New Testament* (Philadelphia: Fortress Press, 1968) for a balanced view, recognizing that gnosticizing tendencies are traceable earlier than gnosticism itself.

[11]E. Andrews, "Gift of Tongues," *The Interpreter's Dictionary of the Bible*, ed. G. A. Buttrick (Nashville: Abingdon Press, 1962), IV, 671-2.

guage. The phenomenon could have developed almost anywhere, but no city offered a better milieu than Corinth.

Problems at Corinth. It can hardly be overlooked that it was in a church where conduct was most disgraceful that tongues were most prized.[12] It does not follow that tongues and disorderly conduct necessarily go together, but at Corinth this was the case. Paul dealt with tongues as a problem, not as a sign of excellence. He did not write to excite the church to further emphasis upon tongues, but to bring the problem under control. In our modern idiom, his intention was to say, "Cool it." One at a time and not more than two or three per service and then only if there was an interpreter, someone to make some sense of it, were his instructions (1 Cor. 14:27).

A rapid survey of 1 Corinthians brings out the extent of the problem at Corinth. Chapters 1—4 deal with the outward problem of division, factions formed around favored heroes, and the inward problem of the world's egocentric wisdom which rejected the wisdom of the cross. In Chapter 5 is the shocking story of incest, a man living with his father's wife. Not only was incest practiced, but the church gloried in it, presumably through some distorted holiness doctrine by which the "spiritual" were thought to be above sin. In Chapter 6 is the ugly practice of lawsuits, as church members sued one another in pagan courts, each trying to get the better of the other. Chapter 7 is an attempt to solve some of the many marital problems which plagued the members of the church. Chapters 8-10 are largely concerned with problems of pride, contempt, and coercion growing out of conflicting ideas about eating meat from a sacrificial animal. Chapter 11 is Paul's attempt to set forth the meaning of the Lord's Supper. This was forced upon him by the calloused indifference of some members of the church toward others, not caring enough for them even to await their arrival before eating. Some over ate and got drunk while others went hungry.

[12]Sidney Cave, *The Gospel of St. Paul* (New York: Harper & Bros., 1929), p. 210.

To skip Chapters 12—14 for the moment, Chapter 15 is Paul's most extensive discussion of the resurrection, this again compelled by serious problems at Corinth. Apparently there were those in the church who rejected the idea of resurrection in favor of "immortality of the soul." Resurrection necessarily refers to the body, or the whole self. The "spiritual," with their gnosticizing tendencies, scorned the body and wanted no resurrection body. They apparently saw themselves as reaching "perfection" through purely "spiritual" means, with ultimate freedom from the body. To them a resurrected body would be a loss, not a gain. Paul, on the other hand, stood squarely in the Jewish understanding of the wholeness of man, created and redeemed in bodily existence.

The threat of tongues. Chapters 12—14 form a unity within 1 Corinthians, and the overriding concern of all three chapters is with "tongues." Paul tactfully couches the problem in the larger consideration of the church as the body of Christ (Chap. 12) and love as the ultimate way of God for man (Chap. 13). It is only then that he comes directly to the problem of tongues, assessing its values and its limitations (Chap. 14).

The three-chapter unit is introduced with a statement about spiritual, that is, charismatic gifts (*charismata*). These are varied, but each is a gift from God. There is to be no selfish pride in these "charismatic gifts," for they are *gifts* of God's grace (*charis*) and not man's achievements. They are not to be competitive, for each has its rightful place, just as each member of the body has its rightful place and function within the body. This opens the way for Paul's beautiful analogy of the church as the body of Christ. Like a body, it must be a unity and it must provide for variety of members within the unity.

Chapter 13 is Paul's beloved "love chapter." It is precisely that, but it is also devoted to the problem of tongues. This is not just a poem or hymn, borrowed from elsewhere and stuck in here. The substance of the chapter may be older than its appearance here, for Paul had in earlier letters written of faith, hope, and love (cf. 1 Thess. 1:3), but in its present form it seems to have been written for this context, Chapters 12—14, and in particular to meet the problem of glossolalia. The whole chapter is illuminated when read from this perspective.

The chapter begins with the limited value and even danger in speaking "with the tongues of men and of angels." An allusion to glossolalia is likely. Mention of "sounding brass and clanging cymbals" is strangely reminiscent of Orphic rites in which ecstasy was sought to the accompaniment of the loud music of bronze cymbals, flutes, and kettle-drums. Exalting love above all charismatic gifts, Paul reserves his most abrupt word for "tongues." Love never ends, and some things give way to higher gifts, like present knowledge giving way to the higher knowledge that is face-to-face encounter. But of tongues Paul says only this, "Tongues will stop" (13:8). They are on a dead-end street, going nowhere. Baby talk, he argued, is appropriate for babies, but when one becomes a man he is expected to put aside the talk of a child for that of a man (v. 11).

In Chapter 14 Paul is conciliatory yet firm. He makes all the room he can for each person and his gift, including tongues; but he raises more warnings and imposes more restraints on tongues than anything else. At best, tongues meet the ego needs of those who practice them: "The one speaking with a tongue builds up himself" (v. 4). This is sharply contrasted with "prophecy," the inspired preaching which "builds up the church" (v. 4). In fact, Paul can justify "tongues" only if there is an interpreter to make some sense of the utterance so that the church may be edified (v. 5).

That tongues at Corinth were unintelligible is conclusive from this context. According to verse 14, tongues do not require the mind (*nous*). It is a "motor reaction," an involuntary utterance resulting from strong emotion but not expressive of the mind. Paul preferred five words spoken with the mind to ten thousand "in a tongue" (v. 19). He had just boasted that he himself spoke in tongues more than all of them. (v. 18). In effect, Paul characteristically met his opponents with the challenge: "Anything you can do I can do better" (see 2 Cor. 11:21 ff. and Phil. 3:4 ff. for his rebuff to those who took pride in observance of the law). But whatever his experience with tongues, Paul restricted it to his private life and did not impose it upon the church (v. 19). Tongues to him were like mere noise from a bugle, giving no meaningful signal to the soldiers who heard it (v. 8). Only the understood word has meaning for the church.

The chief threats of tongues to the church are serious: (1) selfish pride and inadequate goals for one esteeming tongues, (2) denial to the church of a positive ministry of edification, (3) competitiveness and disunity within the church, and (4) alienation of outsiders who would thus see the church only as a madhouse (v. 23).

Corinth not Pentecostal. The contrast between the church in Jerusalem and that in Corinth is striking. When the Holy Spirit came with power upon the church in Jerusalem the results were positive. The disciples were made strong in courage in the face of severe persecution. They preached an understood word and thousands were converted. The church was united and it enjoyed a beautiful *koinonia*, even to table fellowship and the sharing of material possessions. They met daily in prayer, praise of God, study, table-fellowship, and joy. By contrast, at Corinth problems were compounded and intensified by spurious claims to "spirituality." The "enthusiasm" there led to divisions, illicit sex, lawsuits, marital breakdowns, quarrels over personal scruples, disorder at the Lord's Supper, rejection of the resurrection.

Just as the churches at Jerusalem and Corinth were dissimilar, so were the tongues. Modern tongues are not Pentecostal. They are Corinthian. That is not to say that the moral failures of Corinth characterize tongue-speaking groups today. That is not implied here. It is to say that the unintelligible character of modern glossolalia follows the Corinthian pattern and not the Pentecostal one. That pride, competitiveness, and division also closely relate to modern tongues movements seems to be a matter for observation, open to any who care to look.

It is not our purpose here to actively oppose modern "tongues."

Speaking in tongues is the privilege and responsibility of those who choose them. But this writer cannot conscientiously commend modern glossolalia. The New Testament and subsequent history would warn about the extremely limited values in meeting ego needs and the high risks to personal fulfilment and to the unity and serious mission of the church. One can receive as his brother in Christ the one who "speaks in tongues" and at the same time caution him as to its evident hazards. Those who sincerely believe in "tongues" have the right to advocate them, but by the same token those who see the dangers have the right to raise their voices in warning. To practice a form of religion is one thing, to propagate is another. When one enters the religious "market" to sell, he may not cry "unfair" if his wares are challenged. One must reject flatly the notion that "tongues" is a necessary gift of the Spirit or necessary sign that one has been "filled with the Spirit." The New Testament points to other evidencies for this.

Incarnation vs. discarnation. Probably the heaviest charge that may be levied against glossolalia is that it basically is gnostic, a reversal of the mighty event in which the Word became flesh. Jesus Christ was the Word made incarnate; glossolalics try to escape the world of flesh by becoming discarnate. In Jesus the Word penetrated the world of flesh so deeply that it could be seen, heard, and felt (1 John 1:1-3) and to the extent that words like the Beatitudes and the parables were understandable to simple folks. Glossolalics would utter sounds so "unfleshly" or discarnate that only the "interpreters" professed to understand them. Jesus moved deeply into the world with simple, understandable words for the ordinary person, not into some "seventh heaven," uttering uncertain sounds like a mixed-up bugler (1 Cor. 14:8) or to speak in "tongues" so rarified that only the spiritually elite could understand them.

The effort on the part of Corinthian glossolalics to escape the world was not successful. Kaesemann in his comment on Romans 8:26 f. (also 1 Cor. 14; 2 Cor. 12) puts it forcefully: "Far from understanding ecstacies, and particularly the speaking with tongues, as a sign that the Christian community has been translated with Christ into heavenly existence (the view taken by the Corinthian enthusiasts), the apostle (Paul) hears in these things the groans of those who, though called to liberty, still lie tempted and dying and cry to be born again with the new creation."[13]

Kaesemann puts his finger on the most important point in saying, "Just as the incarnation of Christ is the beginning not of man's deification but of his humanity, so the same remains true where it is the spirit that reigns."[14] Christ came not only to make the Word intelligible and accessible at the human level, that of simple people and children, but he came to enable man to become truly man. He did not come to make men divine. Salvation is not becoming an angel, a semi-god, or God. Salvation is God's work of making man an authentic human being, nothing more and nothing less.[15] Where the Spirit enters into a human life, one has the liberty and resources to become human. Tongues move in a direction opposite to incarnation and salvation.

One of the strangest charges made by Paul appears in 1 Corinthians 12:3, "Therefore I want you to understand that no one speaking by the Spirit of God ever says, 'Jesus be cursed!' and no one can say 'Jesus is Lord' except by the Holy Spirit" (RSV). "Cursed" translates *anathema*. Why would Paul have to issue this warning? How could anyone in the church in Corinth possibly say, "Jesus be cursed"?

There is only one background which sheds any light upon this, and it is exactly that of the "enthusiasts" or self-styled "spirituals" at Corinth. It could follow from the gnosticizing there to despise the earthly Jesus in favor of the risen, "spiritual" Christ. Just as

[13]Ernst Kaesemann, *Perspectives on Paul* (Philadelphia: Fortress Press, 1971), p. 134.

[14]*Ibid.*

[15]Cf. my faculty address, "Salvation in the Synoptic Gospels," *Review and Expositor*, Vol. LXIX (Summer, 1972), No. 3, pp. 355-67 and my book, *Polarities of Man in Biblical Perspective* (Philadelphia: Westminster Press, 1973), *passim*.

they despised the idea of a resurrected body for themselves in favor of a bodiless, immortal "soul," so could they despise the humble, bodily Jesus in favor of the glorious, spiritual Christ. With their gnostic disdain for the material as evil, they well could have said, moved by what they thought was the Spirit, "Jesus be accursed!"[16]

To Paul this would be an anomaly, an utter impossibility for one truly moved by the Holy Spirit. To him one could not by the Spirit say "Jesus be anathema." The Spirit would prompt him to say "Jesus is Lord!" and not just "Christ (as distinguished from Jesus) is Lord." This is the very distinction between the earthly Jesus and the risen Christ which John contested in branding it the rankest heresy to deny that oneness of Jesus and the Christ: "Who is the liar except he who denies that the Christ is Jesus" (1 John 2:22). Corinthian enthusiasts, like John's opponents, tried to move away from the historical, incarnate Christ Jesus; and they also tried to move away from the idea of bodily resurrection as well as into a heavenly, unfleshly manner of speech, "tongues" known only to the world-escaping, spiritually elite. Glossolalia at Corinth was not incarnational but discarnational, the "unfleshed word," going even to the extreme of rejecting Jesus for an unfleshed Word.

[16]Cf. Schmithals, *op. cit.*, pp. 124-32.

5 The Holy Spirit and Healing

A more revealing and searching question can hardly be found than that put by Jesus to some who opposed the style of his ministry to human need, "Are you angry with me because I made a whole (*holon*) man well (*hygie*) on the sabbath?" (John 7:23). Jesus had healed a man who for thirty-eight years had been a cripple (5:1-18). Seeing the man in his crippled condition, he asked, "Do you wish to become well (*hygies*)?" Finding the man responsive, Jesus first healed him in body, enabling him to stand up and walk, and then finding him later in the Temple, he healed him at a deeper level, "Behold, you have become well; do not go on longer in sin, lest something worse happen to you" (5:14). Jesus not only healed the man in body but went on to heal him from sin within.

Some who were moved by religious zeal turned on Jesus because it was on the sabbath day that Jesus had healed the man. Two drastically opposed approaches to religion met head on here, as was often the case between Jesus and some of his deeply religious contemporaries. They were concerned to save religion in its institutional expressions: sabbath, food laws, fasting, and so forth. Jesus was no iconoclast out to crusade against these forms, but his concern first and last was with the personal, to save man himself. Religious structures were important to him only to the extent that they served the existence of man. To him, "The sabbath was made for man and not man for the sabbath" (Mark 2:27). This puts in perspective the whole ministry of Jesus.

It was in reply to the continuing opposition to his perspective that Jesus posed the scorching question, "Are you angry with me because I made a whole man well on the sabbath?" Jesus not only put man ahead of religion, but his concern was with the whole man. He came to make the whole (entire) man whole (well). Jesus was more concerned for the inner man than for the outer, but those concerns were not competitive. He protested the religious concern which would wash the outside of the cup or platter only to leave the inside unclean (Matt. 23:25 f.), but never did he endorse the cleansing of the inside alone. His concern was to cleanse both the inside and the outside.

Jesus was not only rejected by some of his religious opponents, but he was also misunderstood by some of his nearest followers at precisely this point. None less than John the Baptist, of whom Jesus said there was none born of woman greater than he, was troubled by the manner of Jesus. In prison at Machaerus because of his open rebuke of the adulterous marriage of Herod Antipas and Herodias, John was sufficiently puzzled by the manner of Jesus that he sent two of his disciples to raise with Jesus the primary question, "Are you the Coming One, or should we await another?" (Luke 7:19). John apparently had expected a different kind of ministry from Jesus, symbolized by the axe laid at the roots of rotten trees, the winnowing fork to separate the chaff from the grain, and the fire to burn up the chaff (Matt. 3:10-12; Luke 3:17). In his reply to John, Jesus pointed to what he was doing: the blind were given sight; the lame walked; the lepers were being cleansed; the deaf were now hearing; the dead were being raised; and the poor were being evangelized (Luke 7:22). Then followed what is perhaps the most neglected beatitude of all: "And blessed is he who is not scandalized by me!" (v. 23).

Jesus was irrevocably committed to a ministry to the whole man. He rejected the expected messianic role, a nationalistic Messiah who would by military force deliver his nation from foreign rule. He had come to save all men and to save each man from his sins (Matt. 1:21). Sin directly or indirectly had damaged man in his total being. Jesus came to free man from all that bound him; to heal man in body, mind, and spirit; and to give him a new and abundant life.

It is against this background that the whole issue of healing is to be considered. Jesus was on the side of life, not death. He was on the side of health, not sickness. He was on the side of food for the hungry, not leaving man in hunger. He was on the side of freedom, not bondage. He was on the side of holiness, not sin. He, indeed, came to make the whole man whole.

Miracles in the New Testament

Miracle stories in the New Testament are far too numerous and significant to be explained away or written off as peripheral as was attempted by the "rationalism" of earlier generations. They are deeply imbedded in the Gospel and Acts, with supportive allusions in the Epistles. References are too numerous to require citation. Alan Richardson is correct in his observation that "the miracle stories do not constitute a secondary *stratum* of the Gospel tradition which is somehow foreign to the *ethos* of the Gospel in its primary sense."[1] To look no farther, 209 verses out of 666 in Mark (to 16:8) relate directly or indirectly to miracles.[2]

Many of the miracles had to do with healing, both of body and mind. People who were lame, blind, deaf, palsied, leprous, feverish, and otherwise suffering from sickness or disease were healed. Another class of those healed were the emotionally disturbed and mentally deranged. These latter included exorcisms of demons, however demons are to be understood, whether separate beings or subjective states of those called demoniacs (see below).

The fact of miraculous cures is far clearer in the New Testament than the motive behind them. Was it compassion, to awaken

[1] Alan Richardson, *The Miracle Stories of the Gospels* (London: SCM Press, 1941), p. 17.
[2] *Ibid.*, p. 36.

faith, to reward faith, to attest to the deity of Christ, or what? It seems that no single motive is implied but rather a complex of motives.

Compassion. It is explicit that Jesus was moved with compassion as he saw people in their various needs and sufferings. When he looked upon the crowds he was moved with compassion, seeing them to be like sheep harrassed and tattered or like an overripe crop about to be lost (Matt. 9:36-38). When the crowds followed him from the towns by foot into the open areas he looked upon them with compassion, healed them, and fed them (Matt. 14:13-21; cf. also 15:32). Jesus is reported also to have had compassion upon individuals in their needs and to have healed them: two blind men (Matt. 20:34), a leper (Mark 1:41). He met a widow of Nain on the way to bury her only son, had compassion upon her, and raised the son (Luke 7:13).

Only in the Synoptic Gospels, and a surprisingly few times, is compassion explicit in Jesus' motives of healing. It does not follow that his compassion went no farther than these instances, but it is clear that this is not the chief motive behind these miracles as presented in the New Testament. The evidences for Jesus' great concern for people goes beyond these few occurrences of the term for compassion, but his compassion obviously did not find its basic expression in such miracles.

It is sometimes said that Jesus never met a sick person whom he did not heal or a funeral which he did not break up by raising the dead. This is well-meaning sentiment, but it does not find support in the New Testament. John reports that Jesus came upon a multitude of sick people at the pool of Bethzatha, some blind, some lame, and some withered; but we read that he healed only one lame man (John 5:1-9).

The evidences are that Jesus did not feed all the hungry, heal all the sick, nor raise all the dead. However, by deed and by word he did reflect the fact that he cared and that he was on the side of life, sustenance, and health. He did command those who have to share with those who have not (Matt. 5:42), and he made the final judgment to rest upon such matters as giving food to the hungry, water to the thirsty, hospitality to the stranger, clothing for the naked, care for the sick, and companionship for those in jail (Matt. 25: 31-46). It is obvious that he did not look to miracles as a substitute for what people can do for one another in terms of provisions which God has made already. He did not prescribe "faith healing" as a substitute for meeting human need through "natural" (God-given) means. That was not even his primary let alone sole solution.

Faith. The New Testament sometimes relates faith to healing and other miracles, but it by no means follows that faith was always so rewarded or that miracles always awakened faith. It is explicit that often faith was not awakened despite acknowledged miracles. Some of Jesus' opponents, for example, acknowledged that he had exorcised demons but on the basis of this accused Jesus of deriving his power from Satan (Luke 11:15). Jesus warned of a heavy judgment upon the cities of Chorazin, Bethsaida, and Capernaum because they had not repented, even though mighty works had been done among them (Matt. 11:20-24). When certain Pharisees asked Jesus to show them "signs from heaven" he refused, for there were no signs which could compel faith in those whose minds were already made up (Mark 8:11-13).

True faith is never compelled by God, and it is evil to seek by "faith" to compel God to act. This is the point of one of the wilderness temptations, when Jesus was asked to throw himself down from a pinacle of the Temple, thus forcing God to keep his promise to save him (Matt. 4:5-7). Jesus rejected as satanic the presumptuous thought of thus by faith attempting to compel God.

On the other side we read that Jesus did on occasion heal in response to faith. To a Roman centurion who pleaded for his sick servant Jesus said, "As you have believed, let it be to you" (Matt. 9:29). A healed and grateful leper was told, "Your faith has saved you" (Luke 17:19). Because of the unbelief of his own people at Nazareth, Jesus was unable there to do any mighty works—except that he healed a few of their sicknesses (Mark 6:5). Presumably, the "mighty works" were other than healing from sickness.

Overall, the New Testament does not offer a single, simple pattern as to faith and healing. Faith sometimes is named as the grounds for healing. Some were healed without prior show of faith or even knowledge of who Jesus was. Many were not healed, although they were not charged with being faithless.

Even where there was faith, there was not always healing. Paul prayed three times for the removal of what he called "a thorn in the flesh," but it remained (2 Cor. 12:7 f.). Whether or not the "thorn" referred to physical illness is not known. Whatever the problem, it remained. Paul was given grace to bear the "thorn." He does not admit to lack of faith. Paul reminded the Galatians that it was because of illness that he first preached to them, presumably because he was too sick to travel on to his intended field (Gal. 4:13). Nothing is said about faith healing for this missionary. At the very close of what may be Paul's last letter, he reports, "Trophimus I left sick in Miletus" (2 Tim. 4:20).[3] Did Paul lack the faith to heal him? Rather, does it not caution us that even where there is even such faith as Paul had, sickness may remain?

Messianic signs. Probably the miracles are to be best understood as messianic signs, or signs of the inbreaking of the kingdom of God. Jesus' first and central message was that the kingdom of God was at hand (Matt. 4:17). He called all men to repentance, a radical turn or conversion from their sinful ways to submission to the kingdom of God. Kingdom means rule, God's kingly rule. Men are first to seek the kingdom of God and his righteousness, all else depending upon that (Matt. 6:33). To the risen Christ was given all authority in heaven and earth, and the

[3]Even if pseudonymous, as viewed by most critical scholars, Paul here is remembered as capable of leaving a friend in sickness. For a thorough study of authorship, with all options seriously considered, see Martin Dibelius, *The Pastoral Epistles.* 4th rev. ed. by Hans Conzelmann. Tr. by P. Buttolph and A. Yarbro, "Hermeneia" (Philadelphia: Fortress Press, 1972), *passim.*

business of his disciples as they go about is to call all nations to submit in obedience to this authority (Matt. 28:18-20).

The kingdom of God is primarily his sovereign rule, and this rule is seen as overcoming the rule of Satan. The miracles are expressions of the power of God, and they foreshadow God's ultimate triumph over all sin and all hostility. This is brought to light in the Beelzebul controversy (Luke 11:14-23).[4] Jesus had freed a demoniac and was accused by some of his opponents of having done so through league with Beelzebul. Jesus pointed out the absurdity of the charge, for Satan would not destroy his own house. Drawing out the true implication, Jesus said, "If by the finger of God I cast out demons, indeed the kingdom of God has arrived" (v. 20).

Two kingdoms met head on, that of God and that of Satan. Healing men of their physical, emotional, and mental ills was a part of God's redemptive work in Christ. These mighty acts meant that the powers which ultimately would have complete victory were already at work in Jesus. The miracles performed by Jesus and his earliest followers are best understood as special acts of God in conjunction with the unique inbreak of his kingdom into the world in the person of Jesus Christ, extended for a time into the work and witness of the church in its formative period. Kallas puts it this way: "Jesus announced that the kingdom of God was coming, and then he dramatically proved it by carving out a small area where the kingdom was present in a localized sense.[5]

The Gospel of John makes explicit and emphatic the understanding of miracles as signs. The term "miracle" translates the Greek *teras*, a word stressing the emotion of amazement or wonder. This term appears often in the New Testament, but never alone. Ironically, the term (miracle) which has come to dominate

[4]Cf. C. K. Barrett, *The Holy Spirit in the Gospel Tradition* (New York: The Macmillan Co., 1947), pp. 59, 62f.

[5]James Kallas, *The Significance of the Synoptic Miracles* (London: S.P. C.K., 1961), p. 78.

in Christian usage is secondary in the New Testament. John's term is sign (*semeion*). He saw the miracles as action parables, an occurrence on one level pointing to a higher level. The feeding of the five thousand pointed to Jesus as the bread of life (Chap. 6). The giving of sight to a man born blind pointed to Jesus as the light of the world (Chap. 9). Raising Lazarus from the dead pointed to Jesus as the resurrection and the life (Chap. 11).

A sign is more than a symbol. Whereas a symbol may be arbitrary and artificial, with no inherent correspondence to that which it symbolizes, a sign has an intrinsically closer relationship to its referent. A ring may be a beautiful symbol for marriage, but it is purely arbitrary. A track made on the ground by an animal is a sign, not a symbol. The track does not just suggest an animal; it bears a direct relationship to the animal that made it.

The miracles of Jesus are more than wonders, and they are more than symbols. They are signs of the actual penetration of God into history at the physical, material level. They are "tracks" of God left as he walked amidst human need. They are actual deeds of God, overcoming evil and its results at one level of reality. They point to the ultimate victory of God in behalf of his people, to a kingdom already inaugurated but finally to be brought to its consummation. As signs, the miracles belong intrinsically to the Gospel, both as proclamation (*kerygma*) of the kingdom and teaching (*didache*) as to its nature, provisions, and demands.[6]

The Commission. Jesus not only healed people but he commissioned the twelve and the seventy to do so. In commissioning the twelve (Matt. 10:5-15), Jesus instructed them first to proclaim the fact that the kingdom of God was at hand. With this they were to heal the sick, raise the dead, cleanse lepers, and cast out demons (v. 8). It is obvious that they did not heal all the sick or raise all the dead, and it is equally obvious that sooner or later all that generation, including the twelve, died. There was a pur-

[6]Cf. Richardson, *op. cit.*, p. 136.

pose in the release at this time of special powers through the twelve, but obviously these miracles were not an end in themselves, else they soon were nullified by the deaths that followed. They were signs pointing to the kingdom of God, already begun and moving towards its consummation.

It may be observed further that the twelve were not authorized to receive pay for their service. Their instructions were: "Freely ye received; freely give" (v. 8). They were to take no gold, silver, or brass, and not even extra clothing, but were to accept the hospitality of those who accepted their service. There was certainly no provision for their amassing wealth through "faith healing." Should we today fulfil the commission of the twelve, we would need to raise the dead (according to Matthew) as well as heal the sick and take no pay for it. This hardly reflects present-day, faith healing life-styles.

The seventy (or seventy-two) disciples whom Jesus sent out received a similar yet more modest commission (Luke 10:1-12). Like the twelve, they were to proclaim the kingdom of God as at hand (v. 9). Also, they were to heal the sick, and this was to be related to their proclamation of the kingdom (v. 9). Again, they were instructed not to take money or other provisions but to rely upon the hospitality of those receiving their ministry. If the commission to the seventy to heal the sick extends to us, so it seems would the instructions to serve without funds or luggage for the road.

In all likelihood the commissions to the twelve and the seventy had symbolic value in addition to their immediate significance. The number twelve could scarcely fail to suggest a reference to twelve-tribed Israel, and seventy was the Jewish number for the nations of the world. The two commissions point to Israel and the whole world, or to the church as the true Israel and the whole world as its mission. The rule of God is to be proclaimed to the whole world, and the miracles served as signs of the inbreak of that kingdom.

Faith Healing Today

It is not necessarily a deficiency in faith or piety to make the obvious observation that there are no miracles today paralleling some reported in the New Testament. No one feeds five thousand men and their families from a lad's lunch. No one raises from the dead a man four days entombed. No one walks on water unaided by aquatic equipment. One may argue whether or not there are miracles today; but clearly there are none in number or kind corresponding to those reported in the New Testament.

There are claims made today for miraculous cures, some under striking circumstances and with amazing results. When these are examined closely, they almost invariably lend themselves to alternative explanations. Pains suddenly disappear; organic function returns to normal, and fevers quickly subside. There is no question here as to God's power to work miraculous cures. The question is not what God can do but what he does. The cures generally cited as "faith healing" may be just that, but there is nothing to compel that conclusion. There are symptomatic malfunctions and pains which can be emotionally or psychologically induced and also overcome the same way.

Frequent claims for miraculous healing are made in cases where physicians had declared a case incurable. These could well be just that, but the evidence is not compelling. To begin with, physicians are not omniscient nor infallible. For them to declare a case medically incurable does not in itself mean that it is medically incurable. It may be only that they do not know the answer, however near or far. A case in point came to world attention at this writing. Jean Haynes, a twenty-two-year-old woman of Coventry, England, had been deaf all her life and her deafness had been declared incurable by physicians. Working in a factory, an allergy which she had caused her to begin to sneeze. The sneezing became so severe that she was moved to another room, but one last sneeze did the trick. She suddenly began to hear. The medical conclusion was that violent sneezing probably had unblocked tubes to her middle ears (Associated Press, Jan. 8, 1973). Under certain circumstances, such a recovery could have been termed a miracle and a shrine for healing could have been erected on the spot. This amazing recovery of hearing came naturally, through violent sneezing.

What is lacking today is compelling evidence of miraculous cures, paralleling some of those reported in the New Testament. At a recent "healing" service in Louisville, Kentucky, there were many who came with ailments and left without them, but not one such case involved a broken bone or an open wound. Each "cure" could have been psychological as well as not.

Christian claims to "faith healing" have the further complication in that similar claims are made by non-Christian religions. Then, too, within Christendom there have probably been as many "cures" attributed to the virgin Mary as to Jesus. "Cures" at Lourdes and elsewhere, attributed to Mary, are as well attested as those attributed to Jesus by confessional groups who attribute no special place of authority to Mary. Followers of Mary are just as credible, and just as open to reassessment, as are others making similar claims for faith healing. That one had certain ailments and was freed from them is demonstrable. What caused them and what cured them is something else, not subject to "proof" or "disproof."

Many Christians of devout faith have no question about God's power to heal, yet claim no such access to that power as will guarantee healing for themselves or for others. They live in the presence of sickness and death, and often the sickness remains and death comes, whatever one's piety or faith. If there are those today who have special access to divine power to heal, they then have tremendous responsibility. There are in the world millions of people who are starving to death. There are many who are blind, deaf, lame, or suffering the almost unbearable pain of cancer. If some have the power, others of us have the list. Let's get the two together.

By coincidence, at the very time a famous "faith healer" drew thousands to a church service in Louisville (many could not get in the building and were wholly ignored as they waited outside in the streets), I was in a meeting in which a large choir of boys sang, most of them totally blind and the others almost blind. These fine young men were doing the best they could with life and were confessing servants of Christ. Why did not our "faith healer" visit these fine boys and give them sight?

Many questions plague the mind as one ponders the claims for faith healing. Why must the healings take place before great crowds? Why are so few healed? Why are no healings unambiguous? Why do some faith healers get rich? Why are so many of God's children left out? Why do the faith healers also die? Given time, the mortality rate is 100 percent, including faith healers and the founder of Christian Science.

I must conclude that God has not given us an "Aladdin's lamp" or "ring" in the form of prayer, guaranteeing us that faith will necessarily be rewarded with health. Surely we are taught to pray for the sick. Surely the likelihood for recovery is enhanced when we open our hearts and minds to God as well as our mouths to medicine. But in his providence God does not guarantee to any of us freedom from sickness or death. It is a cruel injustice to imply that those who suffer and die, including many saintly persons of piety and faith, are really lacking in faith. For "faith healing" it also is an irony that many who are openly wicked live to old age in good health. Sickness is no more a sign of deficiency in faith or piety than health is proof of faith and piety.

Implications for Today

Sickness and death are stark realities, but we need not cower helpless and hopeless before them. There is much that we can do, even if we find ourselves with no shortcuts or assured results. There are at least three areas open to piety and faith in the face of sickness and death: (1) We can gratefully and prayerfully utilize all the resources which God already has given us for life and health. This means faith and medicine. (2) We can offer many compensating services to those who find no escape from illness or impairment. (3) We can seek meaning for ourselves and others despite sickness and death.

Medicine. There is no necessary conflict between faith and medicine. All that we have in terms of medicine and medical skill is the gift of God. The material resources used in medicine and the skills in surgery are gifts of God. It is the part of faith and gratitude to humbly recognize God's gifts, accept them, and put them to the service of man. If one is to reject all this in favor of a shortcut in terms of "faith healing," why not do the same about food? Why not trust God to sustain life without food? It is no more presumptuous to reject the food which God has provided in favor of a miracle than to reject medical resources in favor of a shortcut to health. Each such rejection is not only presumption but ingratitude.

It is not enough to receive God's gift of medical resources. It is a part of piety to assume one's responsibility in the discovery and development of these resources. This is a part of God's original command to us to subdue the earth. Why should there be billions of dollars each year for implements of war but such neglect of medical research that funds have to be begged for it on the streets and from door to door? True piety expresses its faith, gratitude, and responsible concern in many ways, and support of medical conquest over disease is one proper way.

Yet another Christian duty with respect to disease is to work for proper distribution of God's good material provisions among the billions of people in the world. Malnutrition and starvation are widespread. It is not only an irony but a judgment upon us that the people of the world fall into two camps: the starving and the weight-watchers. Poverty and malnutrition in the midst of affluence cannot please him who so identified with the poor. Jesus said, "Blessed are the poor," but he did not say, "Blessed is poverty." He reminded himself and us that man does not live by bread alone, yet he fed the hungry and cared for the sick.

There are sick people and there are medical resources. God's resources belong properly to his people, all of them. It is a right concern that medical care be made accessible to all who need it. Some of us have no power for "faith healing," but there is that which we can do in extending the God-given resources of medical care to the people of the world.

Compensation. There are compensatory services which we can render those who find no escape from illness or bodily impairment. For example, some of us know that we cannot restore sight to the blind, but we know too that there is that which we can do. For one thing, we can share the sight we have. In various parts of the country there are centers for making recordings for the blind. Books, magazines, and papers are read into microphones, recorded on tapes, and made available to blind people throughout the land. Never do there seem to be enough volunteers who will thus share their eyesight with those who are blind.

There are other services, not only to the blind but to all who suffer impairment. Rehabilitation programs, ordinary visitation, and the many services to which any of us could be guided by those who give special attention to the needs of others.

Meaning. The surest promise of Scripture to those who are sick or impaired is not health or wholeness of body through either medicine or "faith healing," but meaningfulness and fulfilment in life. There are those who live daily with pain and impairment and do so indominably. There are those like Paul who pray in vain for the removal of "the thorn in the flesh" but who find strength to endure and meaning for life nonetheless. What Paul meant by the "thorn" is not known to us, and this is well. To us the "thorn" is whatever it is that would rob life of its meaning. It is whatever it is with which we find that we must live. Whatever it is, there is for us as for Paul not only grace sufficient to endure it but to find life meaningful.

I must confess that my own faith is challenged and strengthened far more by one beautiful life lived in daily pain and impairment than by a church house full of "faith healers." All about us are such people. Let no man dare charge that those are not healed in body because they are lacking in faith. Faith is nowhere more clearly pure and strong than in many of God's good people who live in pain yet bear their witness to the goodness of God. Theirs is an authentic faith which gives them the courage to be—to affirm life in the face of sickness and death.[6]

[6]Cf. Paul Tillich, *The Courage to Be* (London: James Nisbet & Co., 1952), *passim.*

6 The Holy Spirit Today

Jesus promised his followers that he would not leave them orphaned (John 14:18), and he promised them that he would make such provision that they could do even greater works than he: "The one believing on me will do the works which I am doing, and greater works than these he will do, because I go to the Father" (John 14:12). The Holy Spirit is not mentioned in this context, and the emphasis is in fact upon the unity of Jesus and the Father. The words Jesus speaks and the works he does are those of the Father abiding in him (14:9-11). There is no division in God here, and Jesus gives assurance that God's work will go on in increasing measure in his disciples.

In the next paragraph, Jesus spells out the provision made for his followers after his departure, promising them "another para-clete" who would be "with you (reminiscent of Immanuel?) for-ever," even "the Spirit of Truth" (14:16 f.). There is no sharp distinction between the promised Paraclete and Christ's own con-tinuing presence beyond his death. His departure is in a real sense his drawing even nearer. His death will not mean that they have lost him: "I will not leave you orphans; I come to you" (14:18). The promised "coming" may be the Parousia at the end of the age, but the context gives equal or even greater weight to another interpretation, that his own presence would be a con-tinuing one, unbroken by his death. Whether under the caption of the Paraclete or the risen Christ, it is the same divine presence.

Taken together, the two succeeding paragraphs, John 14:1-14

and 14:15-31 stress respectively the unity of Jesus and the Father and the unity of the risen Christ and the Paraclete. Together they presuppose and imply the oneness of God, whether known as the Father, Jesus Christ, or the Holy Spirit. The divine presence and power behind the words and deeds of Jesus will be the very power at work in the followers of Jesus, accomplishing ever increasing works in the days ahead.

Jesus' ministry lasted at most for just over three years. The Gospel of John describes annual pilgrimages of Jesus to Jerusalem for the great feasts, and those would imply a ministry of something over three years. The Synoptic Gospels do not supply data for determining the length of Jesus' ministry, but they seem to imply a very short one. Jesus was highly controversial from the outset of his public ministry, and he was soon put to death. Although those few years were packed full with unforgettable words and works, they were too short for the full impact that Jesus had to make upon the world. He traveled but a few miles from the place of his birth, about a hundred at most. He spoke to a limited number of people in the world, although he did address thousands.

The full implications and applications of his message could not possibly have been expressed or indicated in that brief span. Jesus died, and anticipated his death, before all that he purposed to say and do could be actualized. But Jesus did not see his words and works as ending with his death. They would go on through his people, activated, guided, and empowered by God's continuing presence.

Jesus crossed lines between Pharisee and tax gatherer and between Jew and Samaritan, but he did more. He set in motion a movement which must continue to cross lines and crash through dividing walls made by men and defended by men as though God himself had made them. He took the side of the poor, but he did more. He placed squarely upon his followers responsibility for loving concern for the poor. He called sinners to repentance and to submission to the rule of God, but he did more. He charged his followers with the continuation of this basic work.

In these and other ways, Jesus made impact upon the world into which he came, but he commissioned his followers to extend his works into yet greater works, this made possible by his continuing presence.

Implications and Applications

Much that belongs properly to the work of God's people is not spelled out in the New Testament. What God said and did in Jesus of Nazareth is unique, yet Jesus himself indicated that God has yet more light to break and more work to do. Jesus clearly affirmed that his own teaching would not be brought to its fulness in his lifetime: "I yet have many things to say to you, but you are not able to bear them just now" (John 16:12). Already he had amazed them and startled them. Some were so threatened by his teaching that they abandoned him, finding his sayings too hard to take (6:60-66). Some were so threatened and angered that they determined to kill him (Mark 3:6). Not even his own family and his closest disciples were up to hearing him out (Mark 3:31-35).

Teaching. Jesus looked beyond his own ministry of teaching and pointed to its fuller unfolding after his death. He promised "the Spirit of Truth" who would guide "into all truth" (John 16:13). This is God's continuing revelation. God is not dead; he is not emeritus; he is not silent. But with this truth of the continuing revelation of God is the assurance that what God continues to say through "the Spirit of Truth" is built upon what Jesus himself had taught. There is one continuing divine revelation. Let us note two most significant declarations attributed to Jesus: (1) What he says is really what the Father abiding in him continues to say (John 14:10) and (2) what the "Spirit of Truth" will continue to say is rooted in what Jesus said (16:13). There is one God and one continuing divine revelation, extended and expanded, even to this day.

For us today, two privileges and obligations are incumbent upon us, both to give careful attention to the words and deeds of

Jesus as recorded in Scripture and to hear his continuing word to us. God can give his truth today in new forms and shapes and with new implications and applications. The first test as to whether or not it is indeed "the Spirit of Truth" whom we hear today is that of Jesus' own words and work. The Spirit today can guide us into these further truths which Jesus' first followers were not yet able to bear (16:12), but these new truths will be ones compatible with and growing out of what Jesus himself taught by word and deed. This means that we do not have to have a proof text for every divine directive today, but it also means that nothing today is to be attributed to "the Spirit of Truth" if it is not true to the character of Jesus himself. This is the basic criterion by which we "test the spirits to see whether or not they be of God" (1 John 4:1).

Barriers to cross. Jesus crossed difficult barriers. He did so at the risk of his life, and these acts had much to do with arousing the fears and resentment which helped nail him to the cross. Jesus ate with "tax gatherers and sinners" (Luke 15:1). This was a "no no!" in established religious circles. Tax gatherers and others who did not observe the kosher laws, purification rites, and so forth were considered religiously unclean. Jesus rejected this criterion for purity, finding the source of defilement in the attitudes and purposes of the human heart (Mark 7:15-23). Jesus crossed the barriers between Jew and non-Jew, as when he asked a woman of Samaria for a drink of water (John 4:7). In fact, he crossed several lines here in speaking to a woman, a sinful woman, and a foreign woman. Jesus had to go against the piety of his day to cross these lines, but he did it.

It is sometimes observed that Jesus said nothing in terms of race relationships in the form that issue confronts us today. It is observed also that his life was spent in his own little land, with barely any venture outside it. This is all true, but it is to be remembered that Jesus began where he was, and he began crossing the barriers as he met them. His life was soon cut short, before he reached all of the outward barriers separating man from man. But Jesus did bring under judgment all such barriers as men erect to cut off one man from another. Just as he broke down the "middle wall" of separation between Jew and non-Jew (Eph. 2:14), so would he break down all the remaining ones. It is a part of his continuing work or the continuing work of the Holy Spirit to lead us across these barriers today, whether racial, national, provincial, sectarian, or whatever. This does not mean that all men must be alike. It means that where the Holy Spirit is at work today the barriers between man and man fall just as they fall between man and God. Racial segregation and racial discrimination are evils against which great progress has been made, with much yet to do, nowhere more desperately needed than in the churches themselves.

Nowhere is the work of the Spirit more apparent today than in Christians' rediscovery of one another across centuries-old barriers of confessional difference. Windows and doors of communication, fellowship, worship, study, and ministry have been opened, and it is not likely that they will be soon shut, even though some would seem to want to do so. There are reassessments of their own positions within many major religious bodies today. The Scriptures are receiving intensive study in churches which long neglected them. Ministers and laymen in confessional groups which had been out of touch with one another or engaged in actual hostilities are now finding that they have more in common than they have that divides them. There is a deep longing to understand the other, to know one another, to enter into a *koinonia* of giving and receiving.

This does not mean that "convictions" have weakened or zeal has lessened. It does not mean that "denominations" are about to merge into one superstructure. In truth, there is little attention to that today. The concern is not so much with changing these outward structures but with rediscovering our brotherhood within and across these lines. Is not this the work of God's Spirit today?

The dignity of woman. No one has done more for the dignity and freedom of woman than Jesus of Nazareth. There is no indication that he singled out woman for special concern. He simply saw each human being as first of all a person. He saw a woman as a person for the same reason that he saw anyone as a person. While others saw Zacchaeus as a tax gatherer, Jesus saw him as a person (Luke 19:1-10). Others saw a leper first as a leper and shunned him. Jesus saw him first as a person and touched him (Mark 1:40 f.). Accordingly, when Jesus saw a woman, he saw her first as a person and treated her so.

It does not follow that Jesus denied the fact of sexual difference or its significance. Woman's liberation is one thing, but the denial to a woman the right to be a woman in distinction from a man is another thing, just as would be true for a man's right to be a man in distinction from a woman. Distinction or difference does not imply a superior or inferior worth or inequality in value or rights.

It is to be admitted that Jesus did not spell out the implications for the personal dignity and freedom of woman, nor did he include woman in the circle of the twelve. But Jesus did assume an attitude toward woman which opened the way for and compelled gradually unfolding implications and applications. There has come in recent generations, and especially in recent decades, an almost unprecedented break-through in the recognition of woman's rights: the right to vote in many countries, an end to the cruel binding of little girls' feet in the Orient, the opening of wider areas of professional work, challenge to the double standard in morals, equal educational opportunities, and so forth.

In the church as in the world, the dignity and freedom of women are coming gradually to more adequate recognition. In Jesus' day women had no part (unless that of spectator) in the synagogue services and only a limited participation in the Temple services. According to rabbinic teaching, women could not touch the Scriptures lest they defile them. In many respects, woman fared little better than property. Although at his death the attitudes and patterns of the communities had changed little if any with respect to woman, Jesus had reflected an attitude so new and so different that the world could not forever resist that impact.

The adjustment to the attitude and stance of Jesus has come as slowly and painfully within the church as outside it. Woman has had a most restricted place in most of the church through most of the centuries, with significant exceptions. Paul's directives to the Corinthians have received more attention than has the example of Jesus. Paul's instructions for a problem-ridden church in Corinth have been granted more weight than his own great vision that in Christ all are equally precious and distinctions that are important elsewhere are irrelevant there (Gal. 3:28). It is doubtless a witness to the work of the Holy Spirit today that women are being granted a larger place in the life and work of the church.

Paul's prescriptions for Corinthian practice included silence for women in the church (1 Cor. 14:34) and a veil on their heads when they prayed or prophesied, presumably in church (11:4 f.). It is difficult to see how both prescriptions could hold at once: silence and a veil when praying or prophesying, the latter meaning inspired preaching. Also, it is difficult to understand Paul's grounds for commanding women to be silent in church, "just as the law says" (14:34). Elsewhere, Paul had argued that in Christ we are freed from the law (with special reference to the ritual law) and that it was a breach of faith and a betrayal of grace to turn back to the law (cf. Gal. 2:11-21; 3:10-24; 4:5,21; 5:3 f.,18). He resumed this theme in Romans, written soon after the Corinthian letters (cf. Rom. 6:14 f.; 7:4).

When one considers these difficulties plus Paul's great vision that "there is not any Jew nor Greek, not any bondslave nor freedman, not any male nor female, for ye are all one in Christ Jesus" (Gal. 3:28), one wonders if we have sufficient background for understanding these local prescriptions for the Corinthians. One wonders if there may have been some local circumstance, the "silence" regulation referring in particular to "tongue speaking." Another possibility is that the original text of Corinthians may have suffered scribal changes resulting in what appears to be mutually exclusive instructions to wear a veil when praying and preaching and yet keep silence.[1] These prescriptions are peripheral, obscure, and difficult if not impossible to harmonize with Paul's theology as expressed elsewhere. The vision of Galatians 3:28 is clearly stated, and it is not incidental. It gathers up a thread running through all Paul's writing.

Paul carried through forcefully as to his vision that in Christ there is no Jew or Greek. He refused to let circumcision or its absence be a test for salvation or table fellowship. Once at Antioch of Syria he rebuked Peter to his face before the church because Peter and others withdrew from table fellowship where Gentiles were present (Gal. 2:11-14). There is no evidence that he followed through in like manner on that part of the vision which applied to "male and female," and there is some evidence, problematic as it is, to the contrary. But the vision is there. Movement today in the churches toward a more adequate implementation of that vision may well be a part of the work of the Holy Spirit today.

War on war. Throughout the traceable history of man there has been war *upon* war. For the first time in history there seems to be emerging a sustained and broadly based "war" *against* war. It is true that World War I was allegedly "the war to end all war." That the slogan proved to be unfulfilled is somewhat more understandable as more hard data become available, as for example, the seemingly anticipated if not actually scheduled sinking of the Lusitania by heads of states eager to bring America into the war.[2] But now, in part because of the capacity of more than one state through nuclear power to destroy civilization, and hopefully in part because of more enlightened conscience, there is the most discernable commitment yet in world history to find

[1]In 1 Corinthians 14, verses 34-35 appear after verse 40 in some manuscripts. They could have been an early scribal gloss, inserted in different places and finally finding a permanent home after verse 33.

[2]Cf. Colin Simpson, "Lusitania," *Life* (Oct. 13, 1972), pp. 58-80.

an alternative to war.

Here again, it may be that two motives may be seen to be at work: (1) the nonviolent though nonconformist stance of Jesus Christ and (2) the moving of the Holy Spirit today. Surely the first is demonstrable from the New Testament, however neglectful its students and Christ's followers may have been through the centuries and despite a shameful exploitation of the Prince of Peace for the purposes of war. Jesus was a peacemaker. He was on the side of peace. He declared blessed the peacemakers, saying, "Blessed are the peacemakers, for they shall be called the sons of God" (Matt. 5:9). God's children engage in God's work and by this they are known. Never did Jesus say, "Blessed are the war makers."

It is true that various efforts have been made to enlist Jesus in support of war. In recent times S. G. F. Brandon has through forced exegesis pictured Jesus as little short of a Zealot.[3] Who knows, someone some day may picture Albert Schweitzer or Gandhi as warlords! Let it not be forgotten that Jesus from the wilderness temptations to Gethsemane rejected the role of national deliverer, or a militaristic Messiah. Let it not be forgotten that he died with a point of a sword in his side but not with the handle in his hand. Let it not be forgotten that he authorized his followers to give their lives in his name, but never did he authorize anyone to take life in his name. It is a fearful thing so to twist the deeds and words of Jesus as to use him as divine sanction for our own hostilities. Someday those who make Jesus a militarist or a sanction for the use of brute force may have opportunity to explain to Jesus how and why they did it. If we choose to justify war by our logic that is one thing. But to make him our support for war is quite another thing.

Frequent appeal is made to the cleansing of the Temple by those who would use Jesus to sanction brute force. Jesus was angered by the crass abuse of the Temple by religious profiteers

[3]S. G. F. Brandon, *Jesus and the Zealots* (New York: Charles Scribner's Sons, 1967).

and by the denial of its real purpose to the people. He did give outward expression to his feeling, overturning tables of money-changers and driving the cattle out of the Temple court (Mark 11:15-17). Brandon follows the popular notion that Jesus used a whip upon people. This is nowhere affirmed in the New Testament. John alone mentions the whip, and he clearly indicates that it was used with respect to the cattle and not people. John 2:15, often mistranslated, actually says, "and making a whip out of the cords, he cast all out of the temple, both the sheep and the oxen . . . ." [4] The Greek syntax through two conjunctions (*te . . . kai*) clearly interprets "all" as being the sheep and oxen, not the people. The RSV errs along with many other translations, interpolating "with" into the sentence whereas there is no such preposition in the Greek sentence. How bent on forcing Jesus into a role he rejected we must be if first we mistranslate John 2:15 and then jump from a homemade whip (to frighten animals) to the use and sanction of bombs and napalm on people!

In Gethsemane Jesus gave his final rejection to brute force for self-defense. Peter drew a sword and used it on a foe. Jesus rebuked Peter for so doing and warned, "All those taking the sword shall be destroyed (or destroy themselves) by the sword" (Matt. 26:52). The verb *apolountai* is middle voice in form, although it may be passive in effect. If middle the rendering should be, "they shall destroy themselves," if passive "they shall be destroyed." However to be rendered, the truth remains that Jesus gave a dire warning against the use of the sword. Jesus probably meant only that the sword is met with the sword, war with war, and sooner or later the killers are killed. His total teaching would permit a deeper meaning. With the point of the sword one takes the life of another at the physical level; with the handle in his own hand he destroys his own life at a deeper level.

Paul saw clearly that "the weapons of our warfare are not carnal" (2 Cor. 10:4). He went on to affirm his confidence in the

[4]Cf. George Edwards, *Jesus and the Politics of Violence* (New York: Harper & Row, 1972), pp. 64 ff.

power of "spiritual" weapons to overturn the strongholds of evil. Paul learned this from Jesus. Saul of Tarsus had tried by brute force to overthrow what he thought was evil. From Jesus he learned the secret of true power. His faith shifted from the world's brute force as a means to victory or good to Jesus' strange means, exemplified in the cross, the giving of life and not taking it (cf. 1 Cor. 1:18,24). Paul the follower of Jesus, in sharp contrast to Saul the persecutor, suffered injury but did not inflict it. He was beaten many times, was stoned almost to death, and suffered repeated abuse (cf. 2 Cor. 11:23-29). Although he fought hard with tongue and pen, it is not found anywhere that after his conversion he struck anyone or used physical force on anyone or that he sanctioned such means.

That the Holy Spirit today may be taking us back to the New Testament, especially to the teachings of Jesus, is supported by some of the signs of the times. Possibly we are beginning to respond to the Holy Spirit, a part of whose mission Jesus declared to be thus: "That one will glorify me, because he shall receive from me and he will proclaim it to you" (John 16:14).

Poverty. Jesus clearly was on the side of the poor. In saying, "Blessed are the poor" (Luke 6:20) he did not imply that poverty as such is fortunate. He did clearly assume "the proletarian principle," with sympathy for the poor.[5] He likewise warned against the peril of riches, especially in terms of the damage wealth can do to those who have it or seek it. Wealth can become one's god (Matt. 6:24). It can become one's master and make a fool of him (Luke 12:13-21). His first concern was to free man from the tyranny of the material (Matt. 6:25-31). Next he sought to turn the material to the service of people.

Today there is an acute awareness of the problem of poverty in the world. Millions of people have actually starved to death year after year. Yet millions more suffer malnutrition, never having enough to eat. Yet others live at the poverty level, without the

[5]Carl E. Braaten, *Christ and Counter-Christ* (Philadelphia: Fortress Press, 1972), p. 113.

basic material necessities for personal fulfilment. World conscience is beginning to acknowledge that vast wealth in the midst of poverty is an anomaly which cannot be tolerated. Is this awakening conscience not a part of what the Holy Spirit is doing today? The growing protest against complacent wealth in the midst of poverty is not a "devilish plot"; it is the moving of God's Spirit in the consciences of responsible people.

One answer to the problem of hunger is population control. This is a serious proposal made by men of enlightened and responsible conscience. That it is wrong and tragic to spawn children with no provision for their most elementary needs would seem to be a self-evidencing truth. That a "population unlimited" cannot be fed by limited food production is simply to be admitted. But is this the whole answer? What about the hungry people already brought into the world and awaiting food? What about the unborn who have every right to be brought to birth? Is the answer simply that we need less people in the world?

It may be true, as some informed specialists are telling us, that it is impossible to produce enough food to feed the world. One would be more convinced had we ever seriously tried to feed the world. We are not producing to our potential. The wealthiest nation in the world has for decades had a studied policy of limiting production and even of destroying unwanted surplusses. Probably the real potential in food production has scarcely been tapped. Then, too, the food we have has never been shared as it should and could be. Most of us fall into one of two groups: starving or on some weight-watcher's program. One part of the world is starving and the rest is preoccupied with the problem of excess fat. It is a sin that this should be so, starvation and obesity side by side. The simple truth is that the conscience of the world has not yet been sufficiently awakened to the problem of food to undertake seriously to grow enough food or to fairly distribute the food it has. Possibly, at least, the Spirit of God is now stirring that conscience.

Health. Jesus was clearly on the side of health, not on the side of sickness. By his own action and by the commission he gave the twelve (Matt. 10:5-15) and the seventy (Luke 10:4-12), he put that beyond all doubt. Although an isolated few claim direct access to healing powers which they strangely enough employ sparingly, most of us lay no claim to any short cut to health for ourselves or others. However, God has not left us without resources. He has given us brains for research, hands for skilled surgery, and natural resources for nutritious food and curative medicine. God's resources gratefully received and faithfully utilized by responsible people can go far toward overcoming sickness and disease.

Since World War II the United States has spent about two trillion dollars (a trillion is a thousand billion) on the military. The rest of the world combined has spent a like amount. Anything like this amount spent on food production and distribution and on medical research, hospitals, and medical service would radically change the situation as to poverty and health. Growing concern in these directions may attest to some moving of the Holy Spirit as he performs his work today.

Ecology. Jesus taught nothing explicitly in ecology. He did reflect a closeness to nature and a beautiful sensitivity to it. He spent much of his traceable life in the open country, in the fields, and by or on Lake Galilee. He spoke often of birds, fish, flowers, trees, animals, crops, and the soil itself. He did not worship nature, and he clearly placed the value of man above that of animals (Matt. 12:12) and birds (10:31). On the other side, Jesus had no gnostic disdain for nature. He did not see it as evil or worthless. By no word or action did Jesus give support to the world's irresponsible ways of depletion, pollution, or destruction otherwise of God's good earth.

Responsible ecology is not a secular or merely political or economic responsibility. It is a moral and religious responsibility. It belongs to God's first commission, that man, made in the image of God, is to have dominion over all things made. God related creatively to his world, bringing light into darkness and form into formlessness (Gen. 1:1 ff.). Man's likeness to God goes beyond this, but a part of what it is to be in the image of God is to relate responsibly to creation, bringing order out of disorder, light into darkness, and bringing it to its highest production. The world's growing awareness of its ecological crisis and its feeble beginnings in the direction of reversing the trends of depletion and pollution may well be a part of the Holy Spirit's work today. The Spirit of God who moved over the dark waters in the beginning (Gen. 1:2) may be at work today, moving us out of our darkness and chaos.

The Church's Agenda

When Jesus preached in his home synagogue in Nazareth, he began by quoting Isaiah 61:1-2, "The Spirit of the Lord is upon me, because he anointed [Christ] me . . . " (Luke 4:18). He then indicated the direction of his ministry as the anointed one: the gospel for the poor, release to captives, sight for the blind, healing for those wounded, acceptance before God. This "inaugural address" plus Jesus' reply to John the Baptist about his ministry of sight for the blind, strength to walk for the lame, cleansing for lepers, hearing for the deaf, life for the dead, and the gospel for the poor (Luke 7:22), and the whole Gospel account of his ministry should leave us in no doubt as to what Jesus considered to be his work. When the Spirit of God came upon him, this is what he did.

What about the church today? What should be its agenda? If we are led by the Holy Spirit today, should it not follow that the agenda of the church bear some likeness to that of Jesus? With the Gospels before us, can there be any excuse for not understanding the concerns of Jesus? How much of our agenda would Jesus support?

The Spirit of Holiness

The term Holy Spirit consists of two words, the first an adjective and the other a substantive. The latter may be and is used independently, Spirit or the Spirit. The first term may point to the nature of the Spirit as holy or to the work of the Spirit as making holy. There is an unmistakable emphasis in Scripture upon the work of the Spirit as "sanctification" or "holiness," two terms for the same thing. This is the Spirit's work of making man pure, clean, whole.

In some Christian circles the Holy Spirit is thought to be a "second blessing," bestowing sinlessness upon the one who receives the Spirit. One may boast that he has not sinned since that day of "receiving the Spirit," even though years have elapsed. With this may be the claim of being above sin. Of course, neither Scripture nor experience supports this claim to perfection or sinlessness. There are texts taken in isolation which could carry this implication. One example is 1 John 3:6, "No one who abides in him sins; no one who sins has either seen him or known him" (RSV). By itself, in English translation, this seems clear enough. But is is not that simple. Earlier statements in the letter are just as emphatic: "If we say that we have no sin, we deceive ourselves, and the truth is not in us" (1:8).

The seeming contradiction is removed when in the first passage closer attention is given to Greek tense usage: "No one who abides in him goes on in sin, no one who goes on in sin has either seen him or known him." In 1:8 John denies that any of us is sinless. In 3:6 he denies that one can go on in the same old life if he is in Christ. Even here (3:6) the explicit reference is to the Father and not to the Spirit (3:1 f.).

Even though any man's claim to a "sanctification" as a condition of perfection or sinlessness is false, it is God's purpose to make his children holy as he is holy (3:3). Alongside the great gospel truth that God forgives and saves sinners is the equally important truth that his presence in a human life is a purifying one. The word "holiness" appears in a number of Greek and Latin manuscripts in the list of "the fruit of the Spirit"(Gal. 5:22). Most manuscripts do not include the term, and it probably was not original to the text, but surely "holiness," properly understood, does belong to the fruit produced by the Holy Spirit.

We desperately need today a recovery of true holiness. We need a true piety. This does not mean a return to Puritanism or Queen Victorianism. To begin with, there is little chance or danger of that. Piety itself as a model or standard has fallen into such ill repute or is so suspect that many are more disposed to conceal it than reveal it. Piety is not a mark of distinction or a virtue in many religious circles today. To the extent that this is an escape from sham or superficiality, that is gain. But in rejecting the false piety of other days, we well may have "thrown out the baby with the bath water."

It takes little study or reflection to see that our world is in trouble. There is little evidence of a reverence for life itself, and the idea of holiness is almost passe. Never has war been more denounced yet fought more destructively, with such disregard for life, and with the prospect of a war yet so terrible that in a matter of minutes it could destroy the whole world. We have so despised the material world that we have gone far in poisoning, polluting, and depleting it. We now are beginning at least to acknowledge what we have done. Racism has been denounced in theory, yet it continues in practice, an impossibility where human life as such is reverenced. Marriage has always been threatened by betrayal and divorce, but now there seems to be less willingness even to try to save it. We act as though it were a lost cause. Our animality in its sensual, and especially sexual, expression has been exploited by commercial advertising, the cinema from R to triple X, by books and magazines. Words which once were considered so vulgar that they appeared only on the walls of public rest rooms are now flaunted as the indispensable language for the cinema, stage, and much of the printed word.

Where is the hope? Programing may help but is largely hopeless. Must there not be a new birth of decency, of a sense of the sacred, of holiness, of piety that is neither Puritanical nor afraid to break with permissiveness? If holiness is to be recovered, must we not look to the Spirit of Holiness, the Holy Spirit, for the miracle! We are a people of "unclean lips," as Isaiah confessed long ago. We do need to cry out for the "coal from the altar" which will cleanse our lips. Isaiah cried out for such cleansing after "seeing God high and lifted up" and after hearing him acclaimed as "Holy! Holy! Holy!" Do we not need a new vision of the holiness of God and a new openness to him alone who can make us holy as he is holy?

BIBLIOGRAPHY

ANDREWS, E. "Gift of Tongues," *The Interpreter's Dictionary of the Bible*. ed. G. A. Buttrick. Nashville: Abingdon Press, 1962.

BAILLI, JOHN. *The Idea of Revelation in Recent Thought*. New York: Columbia University Press, 1956.

BARRETT, C. K. *The Holy Spirit and the Gospel Tradition*. New York: The Macmillan Co., 1947.

BEHM, JOHANNES. "Tongues, Other Tongues," *Theological Dictionary of the New Testament*. Grand Rapids: Wm. B. Eerdmans, 1964.

BRAATEN, CARL E. *Christ and Counter Christ*. Philadelphia: Fortress Press, 1972.

BRANDON, S. G. F. *Jesus and the Zealots*. New York: Charles Scribner's Sons, 1967.

BROADUS, JOHN A. *The Gospel of Matthew*, "An American Commentary on the New Testament." Philadelphia: The American Baptist Publishing Society, 1886.

CAVE, SIDNEY. *The Gospel of St. Paul*. New York: Harper & Bros., 1929.

DIBELIUS, MARTIN AND CONZELMANN, HANS. *The Pastoral Epistles*, "Hermeneia" Philadelphia: Fortress Press, 1972.

DODD, C. H. *The Johannine Epistles*, "Moffatt New Testament Commentary." New York: Harper & Bros., 1946.

EDWARDS, R. GEORGE. *Jesus and the Politics of Violence*. New York: Harper & Row, 1971.

HAENCHEN, ERNST. *The Acts of the Apostles*. 14th ed., trans. by B. Noble, G. Shinn, R. McL. Wilson. Philadelphia: Westminster Press, 1971.

HOOKE, W. H. "Genesis," *Peake's Commentary on the Bible*. Thomas Nelson and Sons, 1961.

JOHNSTON, GEORGE. *The Spirit-Paraclete in the Gospel of John*, "Society for New Testament Studies Monograph Series," No. 12. Cambridge University Press, 1970.

KALLAS, JAMES. *The Significance of the Synoptic Miracles*. London: SPCK, 1961.

KAESEMANN, ERNST. *Perspectives on Paul*. Philadelphia: Fortress Press, 1971.

KNOX, JOHN. *The Humanity and Divinity of Christ*. Cambridge University Press, 1967.

LAKE, KIRSOPP, "The Gift of the Spirit on the Day of Pentecost," *The Beginnings of Christianity*, ed. F. J. Foakes-Jackson and Kirsopp Lake. London: Macmillan, 1933.

LEIVESTAD, RAGNAR. *Christ the Conqueror*. New York: Macmillan, 1954.

MAUSER, ULRICH W. "One God Alone." Colloquium Paper, The Southern Baptist Theological Seminary. Spring, 1971.

MORTON, A. Q. AND MACGREGOR, G. H. C. *The Structure of Luke and Acts*. New York: Harper & Row, 1965.

RACKHAM, R. B. *The Acts of the Apostles*, "Westminster Commentaries" London: Metheun and Co., 1939.

RICHARDSON, ALAN. *The Miracle Stories of the Gospels*. London: SCM Press, 1941.

RICHARDSON, CYRIL C. *The Doctrine of the Trinity*. New York: Abingdon Press, 1958.

ROHDE, ERWIN. *Psyche*. trans. by W. B. Willis from the 8th German ed. New York: Harcourt, Brace and Co., 1925.

SCHMITHALS, WALTER. *Gnosticism in Corinth*. trans. by John E· Steely. Nashville: Abingdon Press, 1971.

SIMPSON, COLIN. "Lusitania," *Life*, October 13, 1972.

STAGG, FRANK. *The Book of Acts: The Early Struggle for an Unhindered Gospel*. Nashville: Broadman Press, 1955.

_____. "Matthew," *Broadman Bible Commentary*. Nashville: Broadman Press, 1969.

_____. *Polarities of Man's Existence in Biblical Perspective*. Philadelphia: Westminster Press, 1973.

_____. "Salvation in the Synoptic Gospels," *Review and Expositor*. LXIX, Summer, 1972.

_____, HINSON, E. GLENN, AND OATES, WAYNE E. *Glosso-lalia: Tongue Speaking in Biblical, Historical, and Psychological Prespective.* Nashville: Abingdon Press, 1967.

TILLICH, PAUL. *The Courage to Be.* London: James Nisbet and Co., 1952.

VON RAD, GERHARD. *Genesis, a Commentary.* 2nd ed. rev., trans. by J. H. Mahs. London: SCM Press, 1963.

WAINWRIGHT, A. W. *The Trinity in the New Testament.* London: SPCK, 1962.

WILLIAMS, R. R. *The Acts of the Apostles*, "The Torch Bible Commentaries." London: SCM Press, 1953.

WILSON, R. McL. *Gnosis and the New Testament.* Philadelphia: Fortress Press, 1968.